Editorial Planning and Layout   *Tim Healey*
Co-ordinating Editor   *Verity Weston*
Managing Editor   *Anne Furniss*
Design Consultant   *Peter Benoist*
Production   *Rosemary Bishop*
Picture Research   *Jennifer Golden*
Adviser   *Michael Tregenza*

First published 1978
Macdonald Educational Ltd
Holywell House
Worship Street
London EC2A 2EN

ISBN 0-382-06300-7
Published in the
United States by
Silver Burdett
Company, Morristown, N.J.
1979 Printing
Library of Congress
Catalog Card No. 79-64164

Illustration credits
Key to the position of illustrations: (T) top,
(C) centre, (B) bottom, (L) left, (R) right.

Photographs and prints
American History Picture Library 17(T) (TL),
   21(B), 50(B)
Archiv Gerstenberg 23(B), 24(T)
Associated Press 7
British Library, frontispiece engraving from
   B. B. Hardinge 'Belle Boyd in Camp and
   Prison' volume I, 1865.
Camera Press 44(B)
Crown Copyright/The Man Who Never Was, by
Ewen Montagu, Evans Bros, 1953 36(B)
Stewart Durant 31(T)
Stanley Gibbons 32(TL)
Neil Grant's 'Spies and Spying', Kestrel Books,
   1976 55(T)
Historical Picture Service 15(TL)
Imperial War Museum 31(TR), 32(B), 34(BL),
   55(TR)
Keystone Press Agency 43(C), (BR), 44, 49(T),
   (C), 55(BL), 59(T)
Mansell Collection 11(B), 14(T), (B), 15(TR),
   28(B)
Mary Evans Picture Library 22(B)
Military Museum of the Yugoslav People's
   Army 27(B)
Musée de l'Armée, Bruxelles 31(BR)

Musée de Versailles/Service de
   Documentation Photographique de la
   Réunion des Musées 19(TR)
National Portrait Gallery 13(B)
Neue Arschifte 22-23
Novosti Press Agency 24-25
J. Piekalkiewicz 33(BR), 34-35
Popperfoto 38(B), 38-39, 41(T), 42(T), (B), 45(B),
   49(BL), (BR), 53(T), 56(B)
Public Record Office 12(C)
Radio Times Hulton Picture Library 19(TL),
   25(T), 26(T), 28(T)
Rijksinstituut voor Orloogsdocumentatie 35(T)
Roger Viollet 29(T)
Claus Schulte 51(BL)
Snark International 6, 34(TL)
Society of Apothecaries 13(T)
Suddeutscher Verlag 40(T), (B)
U.S. National Archives 29(B)

Artists
Peter Archer 36-37
Ron Hayward Associates 8(L), 9(L), 12, 16,
   19(TR), 20, 28, 34(TL), 37(TR), 39, 47, 51
Richard Hook/Temple Art 8-9
BL Kearley Ltd 27, 43, 45, 46, 48, 50(BR), 52-53
Peter North 10(T), 29
Jan Parr 15, 54(L)
Temple Art 18, 23, 30-31
Michael Tregenza 40-41, 56-57

TIMESPAN SPIES

WRITTEN AND DEVISED BY TIM HEALEY

CONTENTS

Introduction

Probably everyone has heard spy stories, either about glamorous agents equipped with fantastic devices, or about shady characters fighting out secret wars in the back streets of modern cities. But did you know that Julius Caesar invented a cipher for writing out secret messages? That Mary, Queen of Scots was brought to her execution by the cunning of a great Elizabethan spymaster? Or that Napoleon valued a single spy at as much as 20,000 soldiers?

Spying (or espionage) is the business of gathering and passing on secret information (intelligence). It is a very ancient craft. The earliest human records contain accounts of espionage missions. The Bible includes several such tales. Allen Dulles, a modern chief of America's powerful Central Intelligence Agency was fond of remarking that God Himself was the first spymaster, for according to the Old Testament, God advised Moses to send spies into the land of Canaan.

In Egypt, archaeologists have found a tablet dating back to 1370 BC, on which a Hittite prince asks for an intelligence report on the widow of Tutankhamun. Much, much later, the legends of the Anglo-Saxons in Britain describe how King Alfred disguised himself as a minstrel in order to get inside the camp of the Danes and spy on their defences.

In Ancient China, spying developed into a fine art. Here, a certain general called Sun Tzu wrote a book called *The Principles of War* some 2,500 years ago. He devoted great attention to the importance of spies. They could be divided into five classes, he said: local spies (local inhabitants who may be bribed for information); inward spies (traitors in the enemy's forces); converted spies (captured agents who have been persuaded to change sides); doomed spies (agents used to feed the enemy with false information, and who will probably be killed afterwards); and surviving spies (trained agents who can be relied on to return from their missions).

Sun Tzu's book was so thorough that a simplified version was issued to the Royal Air Force in Ceylon (now Sri Lanka) during World War Two. It suggests how complicated the world of espionage can become. Besides spies themselves, the secret craft breeds spymasters and spycatchers, double agents and agents who supply false information. In real life, it is seldom a glamorous world. Today, spying has become a major industry, and modern intelligence agencies employ thousands of people to sort through information, as other government departments do. The work is often dull and routine.

Yet the great game of espionage is still a fascinating one, as this book will show. Great attention has been paid to spying in the 20th century, but the early chapters also describe several episodes from the span of history. As we have seen, spies are as old as secrets.

▲ Roger Moore as James Bond, agent 007, the glamorous hero of Ian Fleming's spy thrillers.

Facing page: "Silence! The enemy is after your secrets." A French poster of World War Two warns of the danger from spies.

Spies of the Ancient World

Ancient Greece and Rome

▲ According to the Greek historian Herodotus, a certain Histaeius once sent a secret message by shaving his slave's head, pricking out a message on the skin, then waiting for the hair to grow again. The slave carried the message and the mission was a success.

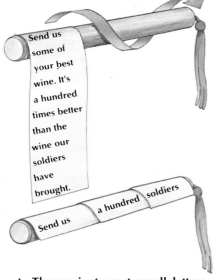

Send us some of your best wine. It's a hundred times better than the wine our soldiers have brought.

Send us a hundred soldiers

▲ The ancients sent scroll letters wrapped around staffs. Alexander the Great invented a way of conveying secret messages by phrasing his letters with care. The method is shown in the diagram above.

In the year 203 BC, a Roman army was besieging the camp of their enemies, the Numidians. The Roman general, Scipio Africanus, was anxious to get a close look at the Numidian defence works before launching his main attack. He decided to send in spies. The plan was simple: he gathered together a small force of his most trusted officers and placed them under the command of his close friend Laelius. Laelius was to enter the camp pretending to sue for peace. The officers were to be disguised as his slaves. The Romans knew that their enemies would be suspicious of anyone wearing army uniform.

Laelius and his "slaves" did enter the camp, and started the peace negotiations. But the Numidians were wary of the Romans and kept them in the centre of their camp, well away from their defence works. The negotiations dragged on, and still the Romans had not managed to achieve the real aim of their mission. Laelius was sitting pondering the problem, when one of the horses in the compound suddenly neighed and reared up, perhaps bitten by a fly. This gave Laelius an idea. He told his "slaves" to move in among the herd of horses and pretend to quieten them down, but really to stir them up and stampede them towards the defences. The plan worked. The spies chased after the startled herd and followed them deep into the Numidian defence works.

Peace negotiations were broken off the next day. Armed with their knowledge, the Romans were able to destroy the enemy defences and invade their camp. The Numidians were routed.

The story of Laelius is told by the Roman historian Frontinus. It is just one of many accounts of undercover missions to be found in the records of Ancient Greece and Rome. It features two of the commonest espionage methods: disguise and deception.

The ancients also devised a number of codes and ciphers to prevent secret information from falling into enemy hands. A code is a pre-arranged group of words, letters or symbols which have an agreed meaning. A simple sentence, "It is raining," may be agreed to mean "Attack now," for example. A cipher is a way of rearranging the whole alphabet according to some agreed system. Julius Caesar invented a simple cipher which has been known as the "Caesar Cipher" ever since.

Counter-espionage is the business of seeking out and stopping enemy spies. The Macedonian Alexander the Great started one counter-espionage practice that has become standard in modern warfare. In 334 BC, he was besieging a Persian town. At first, he would not let his troops write home in case their letters were intercepted and revealed details of his position. Then he began to hear that his troops were discontented. He wanted to find out why, and whether any plots were being hatched. He lifted his ban, and allowed his troops to write home. They did so, but the couriers took the letters straight back to Alexander who had them carefully examined. This is the first recorded example of "postal censorship". (As no plots were discovered, Alexander wisely set about settling his men's grievances.)

THE CAESAR CIPHER

Caesar wrote out an ordinary alphabet, then wrote out the cipher alphabet, below. The cipher was just an ordinary alphabet, but with each letter shifted three places along. Look below each letter of the alphabet for its cipher equivalent:

Alphabet: A B C D E F etc
Cipher: D E F G H I etc

To put the word SPIES into cipher, for example, S becomes V, P becomes S, I becomes L, E becomes H and S becomes V. Thus SPIES reads VSLHV.

Letters may be shifted more or less than three places, but a Caesar cipher is still easy to solve if you use the following "scanning" method.

This message is in a Caesar cipher: "TXQZE LRQ". Under each letter of the cipher, write down the next letter of the alphabet. Sooner or later, the clear message will emerge:

TXQZE	L R Q
UYRAF	M S R
VZSBG	N T S
WATCH	OUT

Problem: Use the method described to solve "FDYIVK OCZ ZHKZMJM".

The Holy Terror

The Spanish Inquisition

▲ The Inquisition was run by monks of the Order of St Dominic. They employed thousands of people from outside the Church as spies and informers.

"Be it noted that the spy, simulating friendship and seeking to draw from the accused a confession of his crime, may very well *pretend* to be of the sect of the accused, but he must not *say* so, because in saying so he would at least commit a venial sin, and we know that such must not be committed upon any grounds whatever."

This discreet advice to spies is taken from a manual published by the Spanish Inquisition. The dungeons and torture chambers of the Inquisition are well known. But it is not often realized that the Inquisition was one of the first organizations to impose widespread "social espionage" on a whole population.

"Social espionage" is day-to-day spying on ordinary people. It is a way of making sure that everyone accepts the authority of a country's rulers. Anyone who holds different views from the accepted ones, must be reported to the authorities and punished accordingly. In recent times, dictators such as Hitler, Stalin and Mussolini have used such methods to hold on to power. The Spanish Inquisition used the same methods to maintain the authority of the Catholic Church.

The Inquisition was first set up in the Middle Ages. It was revived in Spain in 1478 to wipe out heretics (people who do not follow the accepted religious practices). Newly converted Jews and Moors were the first to suffer, but soon the whole population of Spain came under the watchful eye of the Inquisition.

The Inquisition was composed of small bands of Church officials who employed huge numbers of spies and informers to help them in their work. The spies were given special privileges: they were excused paying taxes and could not be brought to trial in ordinary courts. Understandably, their numbers grew quickly. Some local Inquisitions came to employ over a thousand such spies, watching out for the slightest heresy.

Besides the army of official spies, the Inquisition made everyone an unofficial spy. People could be punished for *failing to report* a heresy, as well as for committing one. They began to report on their neighbours for the most trivial offences. The lists of reported crimes were huge. These are just two examples: one 80-year-old man was denounced by a former friend for eating bacon and onions on a day of abstinence, and a woman was reported for smiling when she heard someone mention the Virgin Mary.

Some people denounced their neighbours just to settle old scores. Others became so terrified that they denounced themselves, often for things that they had never done.

Accusations were made in secret, and torture was often used to extract a confession. Condemned prisoners were given their sentences at a grim public ceremony called an *auto da fé* (act of faith). At the end of the *auto*, the least fortunate were taken away to be burnt at the stake. If they confessed at the last moment, they were usually strangled before the flames were lit.

PRIEST HOLES

▼ Inside Catholic Spain, Protestants were cruelly persecuted by the Inquisition. But Catholics in Protestant countries were often treated just as badly. Catholic families sometimes built secret rooms in their houses to hide their priests when danger threatened.

These two examples of secret priest holes are both in Hardwick Hall, County Durham. A "stone" wall swings open to reveal one secret stairway, and a wooden panel tilts to reveal another.

▼ A torture chamber of the Spanish Inquisition, as depicted in an 18th century print. On the right, a victim is hoisted by the *garrucha* (a pulley). In the background, another submits to the *toca* (water torture). A third is tortured by fire, whilst a monk records their forced confessions.

Spies on a Shoestring

Elizabethan Spies

▶English ships defeat the Spanish Armada, 1588. Sir Francis Walsingham had spies in Europe who told him of the Spanish invasion plans. He also had agents among the shipbuilders in the different ports where the Spaniards built their fleet.

DEAD LETTER BOX

▲The code paragraph forged by Walsingham's cipher expert.

◀A "dead letter box" is a hiding place for secret messages. Mary Queen of Scots and her supporters hid their coded messages in the hollowed out bungs of beer barrels. Walsingham discovered the trick and so was able to read their correspondence over a period of three months.

In 1586 Mary, Queen of Scots, was under arrest in England, as Elizabeth I considered her a threat to the English throne. Mary was in contact with certain Catholic conspirators who wanted to overthrow the Protestant Queen Elizabeth. These conspirators managed to keep in touch with Mary by hiding messages in beer barrels which were taken to the house where she was imprisoned. Mary placed her replies, carefully written in cipher, in the empty barrels.

A man called Gilbert Gifford organized this deception. But Mary did not know that Gifford was really a double agent. He was in the pay of Sir Francis Walsingham, the head of the English Secret Service. Every one of Mary's letters was taken straight to Elizabeth's cunning spymaster.

Walsingham followed the secret correspondence, but he did not pounce at once. He was waiting for real evidence against Mary. It came in July 1586. Mary's supporters wrote that they were planning a great Catholic rebellion. Six gentlemen, they said, were ready to kill Elizabeth and put Mary on the throne.

Walsingham wanted to find out the names of these "six gentlemen". Instead of charging Mary at once, he got his cipher expert to forge an extra paragraph in Mary's reply: "I would be glad to know the names and qualities of the six gentlemen who are to accomplish this designement, for it may be that I shall be able, upon knowledge of the parties, to give you some further advice." The names were never needed, for soon afterwards the plotters panicked and gave themselves away. Mary herself was executed.

▲Sir Francis Walsingham (1532-90). Financing the Secret Service was a costly business. At his death, his secretary calculated that the Queen owed him £346 two shillings and sixpence.

After his death a Spanish spy in England wrote to Philip II: "Secretary Walsingham has just died, at which there is great sorrow here." Philip wrote a wry comment in the margin of the report: "There, yes. But it is good news here."

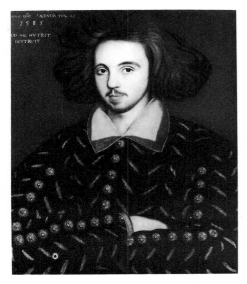

▲ Christopher Marlowe (1564-93). As a young man, this English playwright was employed by the Secret Service. He was one of many students sent by Walsingham to spy on Catholic plotters abroad.

His death is shrouded in mystery. He was supposedly killed in a tavern brawl. But his killer, Frizer, was for some reason given a free pardon. And a Secret Service agent, Robert Poley, was on the premises at the time . . .

Walsingham was the first great English Secret Service Chief. He was loyal and energetic. He also kept a strict account of his expenses. He had to, for although Queen Elizabeth was a brave and shrewd ruler, she was miserly. Walsingham ran his service on a shoestring budget but nevertheless managed to employ spies abroad as well as at home. It was from his agents in Europe that he began to receive reports of a new threat to the throne. Philip II, the Catholic King of Spain, was now making plans to invade Britain.

Sir Edward Stafford, the English ambassador in Paris, sent valuable reports about the invasion plans. He was an English Catholic, and had been one of Mary's supporters. Walsingham had long suspected him of being a traitor. But instead of having him killed, Walsingham "turned him round" (persuaded him to work against his own side). Stafford became a double agent. He set to work gathering information from the Spaniards. At the same time he fed them with false information about England's readiness for war.

Another English Catholic, Anthony Standen, was even more valuable. He used the cover name of Pompeo Pellegrini. Operating from Florence, he managed to get hold of a complete list of the ships, sailors, soldiers and stores which were being collected for the Spanish invasion fleet, known as the Armada.

In 1588, England was ready. The Spanish Armada was sighted exactly where Walsingham had predicted. Precise details about its strength were already known. But Walsingham was now a sick man. Two years after the English victory, he died, hopelessly in debt.

Knight and Lady

The Chevalier d'Éon

▲ D'Éon as "Lia de Beaumont" the beautiful French girl who captured the heart of the Russian court. D'Éon spent his last years in England entirely in woman's disguise. His companion in old age was a Mrs Marie Cole. The results of the medical examination came to her as a dreadful shock. She thought she had been living with another woman.

▲ D'Éon in his Dragoon's uniform. After his successful mission to Russia, he was rewarded by being made a Captain of Dragoons before being sent to England. When he agreed to sign the contract of 1775, he was allowed back into France as a woman. Sometimes he rebelled against the contract and wore his Dragoon's uniform in public; he was imprisoned for three weeks as a result. Disillusioned, d'Éon returned to England where he spent his last years.

On 21 May, 1810, an old French lady known as "Mademoiselle d'Éon" died in poverty in London. To settle the arguments that still surrounded her, doctors examined the body. Four days later, *The Times* published the startling news: "Mademoiselle d'Éon" was a man.

D'Éon's story is one of the strangest in the history of espionage. He began his career as a spy in the service of the French King Louis XV in 1756. Louis sent him to Russia to arrange a secret treaty with the Russian Empress. Since her ministers were suspicious of Frenchmen, d'Éon went in disguise, as a French woman. The lovely "Lia de Beaumont" became a great success at the Russian court, and it was said that many fine portraits were painted of "her." Meanwhile, "the lovely Lia" was successfully concluding the treaty with the Empress, which "she" smuggled back to France.

In 1762, Louis found another job for his talented agent: d'Éon was sent to England to assist the French ambassador there. This time, d'Éon went as a man under his real identity. But he was still employed as a spy. His main task was to find out the state of England's readiness for war, for Louis XV had secret plans to mount an invasion. D'Éon performed his services so well that he was soon made a Chevalier (Knight) and had hopes of being made ambassador. He was a popular figure in English high society. He entertained lavishly and fell into debt.

But Louis began to fear that his spy, who possessed so many secret documents, might be exposed. D'Éon was not made ambassador, but ordered back to France. He grew resentful. A feud broke out between him and the new ambassador, a man called Guerchy. Guerchy made several attempts on d'Éon's life, involving drugs, assault and kidnapping. But d'Éon survived. He fortified his home in Brewer Street, Soho, with a garrison of armed men. He placed explosive mines in his sitting room, bedroom and study. He sealed up his secret documents in the wall of one of the rooms.

The feud became public knowledge and the London mob took d'Éon's side, jeering Guerchy in the street and smashing the windows of his house. Guerchy was called back to France, a broken man. D'Éon himself stayed in England, but the feud seems to have sent him slightly mad. He began to wear women's clothes in public. Rumours began to spread, and bets were even made on his true sex.

In 1774, Louis died, and the French government wound down his Secret Service. But d'Éon would not return his secret documents; he demanded money for them. The spy was blackmailing the new King of France. In 1775, the playwright and adventurer Beaumarchais was sent to England to end the affair. After long drawn-out negotiations, d'Éon agreed to return his documents if the French Government would pay off his debts and let him return to France. Beaumarchais agreed, but on one condition: d'Éon should stop all the scandalous gossip by publicly swearing to being a woman, and he should wear women's clothes for the rest of his life.

▲ Caron de Beaumarchais (1732–99), author of *The Barber of Seville* and the *Marriage of Figaro*. He was also an agent of the French Secret Service.

After concluding negotiations with d'Éon, Beaumarchais went on to smuggle arms to American revolutionaries, under the "cover" of the firm Roderique Hortalez et Cie.

▼D'Éon was a brilliant swordsman and gave fencing displays after his return to England. This picture shows a famous duel at Carlton House in 1787. Here, at the age of 59 and hampered by women's clothes, d'Éon fought and defeated the outstanding swordsman the Chevalier de Saint George. The audience included the Prince of Wales.

"*Since leaving off my uniform and my sword I am as foolish as a fox who has lost his tail! I am trying to walk in pointed shoes with high heels, but have nearly broken my neck more than once. It has happened that, instead of making a curtsey, I have taken off my wig and three-tiered head-dress, taking them for my hat or my helmet.*"

d'ÉON, 1777

▲ D'Éon complained hotly about being made to wear women's clothes forever.

►Man or woman? A print of d'Éon, made at a time when huge bets were placed on the subject.

The Culper Ring

The American Revolution

THE ROUTE OF THE CULPER RING

▼ 1. *Robert Townsend* ("Samuel Culper Junior") collected information from his spies in New York. 2. *Austin Roe,* a daredevil horseman, sped across Long Island with the news. 3. *Caleb Brewster,* a boatman from Fairfield, collected the information and carried it back across Long Island Sound. At Fairfield (4), *Major Benjamin Talmadge* ("Mr John Bolton") assessed the information and sent it on to General Washington, via a series of mounted Dragoons posted at every 24 kilometres (5).

Brewster's job was risky. He beached his boat at different coves on Long Island to avoid suspicion. A certain Anna Strong would hang a black petticoat on her line as a code signal. The position of the petticoat indicated to the Ring where the boat had landed.

In 1775, war broke out between Britain and her American colonies. The British quickly occupied New York and neighbouring Long Island. Soon afterwards, they captured an American spy called Nathan Hale, whose courageous last words from the scaffold have made him the most famous spy in American history. "I only regret that I have but one life to give for my country," he said.

Hale's death made the American leader George Washington determined to set up an efficient Intelligence service in the area. It was run by two men who had been friends of Hale, Major Benjamin Tallmadge and Robert Townsend, and was known as the "Culper Ring," for Townsend used the name "Samuel Culper Junior".

A coded letter, written by Washington in 1778, gives an idea of the kind of information he was interested in: "Mix as much as possible among the officers and refugees, visit the Coffee Houses and all other places . . . find out . . . whether any works are thrown up on Harlem River, near Harlem Town, and whether Horn's Hook is fortified. If so, how many men are kept in each place, and what number and what sized Canon are in those works."

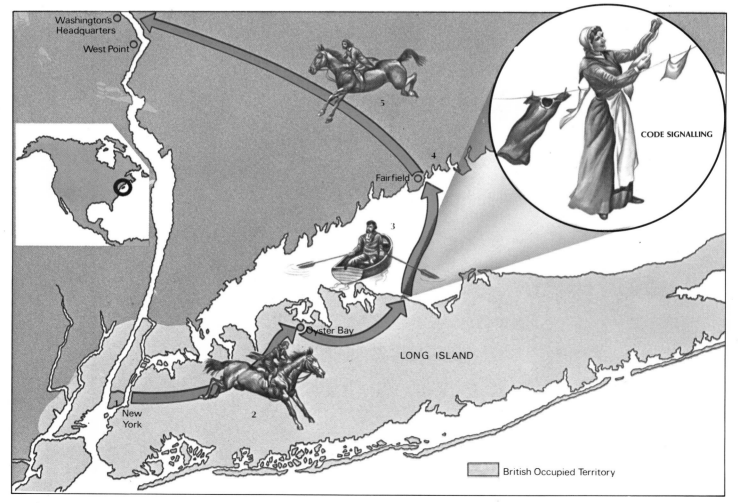

Washington's Headquarters

West Point

CODE SIGNALLING

Fairfield

New York

Oyster Bay

LONG ISLAND

British Occupied Territory

The Culper Ring did not just pass on information. They were also involved, by chance, in the discovery of a British agent called Major John André, in 1780.

British troops had occupied Oyster Bay on Long Island. Several British officers were quartered in Townsend's own house there. Townsend's sister, Sarah, discovered that one of the officers was receiving letters under a false name, that of "John Anderson". The officer's real name was Major John André, and Sarah grew suspicious. She became more suspicious still when she overheard Major André asking for detailed information about the American stronghold of West Point. She informed Tallmadge that André might be a spy.

However, Tallmadge had already received a letter from the American general Benedict Arnold at West Point. Arnold asked him to provide an escort to and from West Point for a friend of his—a Mr John Anderson! Was Arnold seeking contact with a British agent? Was he, an American general, a traitor?

Tallmadge quickly set his men on André's tracks. He was too late, for André had already reached West Point and got in touch with Benedict Arnold. He was already making his way back through the lines with a secret message addressed by Arnold to the British. Luckily, three American militia men suspected him and put him under arrest. André was put on trial and executed as a spy.

Meanwhile, however, the treacherous general Benedict Arnold had managed to escape as soon as he heard that André had been arrested. André was just a courier, the real villain had got away. Townsend himself wrote shortly afterwards that André was "a most amiable character" and regretted that he had been executed. But of the treacherous Benedict Arnold, he wrote "his name will stink to eternity".

▲ **The arrest of Major André (an early print). He carried this pass, obtained for him by Benedict Arnold, and made out in the name of Mr John Anderson.**

▼ **In his boots, André carried a message from Benedict Arnold to the British. In it, Arnold offered to betray the stronghold of West Point for "twenty thousand pounds Sterling". An extract is shown below.**

"If I point out a plan of cooperation by which J.H. shall possess himself of West Point, the Garrison, etc., etc., etc., twenty thousand pounds Sterling I think will be a cheap purchase for an object of so much importance. At the same time, I request a thousand pounds to be paid my Agent—I expect a full and explicit answer—This 20th I set off for West Point. A personal interview with an officer that you can confide in is absolutely necessary to plan matters..."

The Emperor of Spies

Napoleon's Master Spy

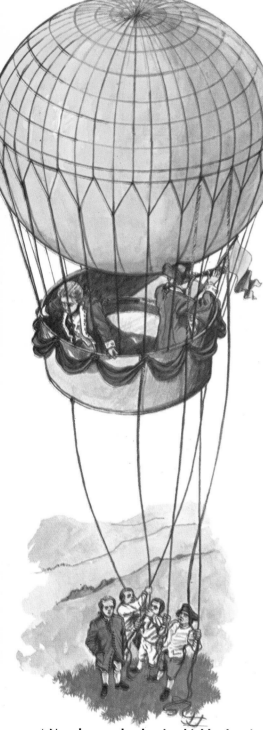

▲Napoleon valued spies highly, but in one respect he lacked foresight. The revolutionary army which he took over had formed companies of *aerostiers* (balloonists). Napoleon did not recognise their value to military intelligence, and disbanded them.

Austria was at war with France. The forces of the French emperor Napoleon were drawn up along the River Rhine and poised to attack. In Austria, a strong garrison manned the strategic fortress of Ulm which guarded the road to Vienna, Austria's capital city.

It was to Vienna that a young Hungarian nobleman came, late in 1804. He was a handsome and elegant man and soon became a popular figure in Viennese society. He also won great sympathy, for his was a sad story. Napoleon had expelled him from France and he had lost everything in his flight. There were many who felt that the young man might prove useful to the Austrian cause, for he had a good knowledge of the state of France and of her armed forces. In time, he was introduced to Marshal Mack, leader of the Austrian army.

Mack was impressed by the young nobleman's grasp of the military situation; so much so that he took him on to his staff and made him Chief of Intelligence. It was a welcome appointment, for this "young nobleman" was Napoleon's master spy, Karl Schulmeister!

Schulmeister set to work at once, feeding the Austrian leader with false information. He claimed to have learned that the French army was in a state of collapse. He produced forged letters from supposedly mutinous French troops. He bribed two Austrian staff officers, Wendt and Rulski, to feed Marshal Mack with similar stories. Napoleon even had special newspapers printed in France, which seemed to confirm the reports.

Mack was completely taken in. Believing that the mutinous French troops were retreating behind the Rhine frontier, he led a force of 30,000 men out of the vital fortress at Ulm. He was hoping to make short work of Napoleon's "crumbling army".

It was then that the French struck. Marshal Ney advanced on the Austrians from the front. Generals Marmont and Lannes closed in on one flank. Generals Soult and Dupont closed in on the other. Mack might have withdrawn at this point, but there was Murat, closing in from behind. Sealed off from retreat, the Austrians surrendered. The almost "bloodless" victory was decisive. Less than a month later, the French took Vienna and occupied that city for the first time in history.

It was Schulmeister's greatest coup, but not his only one. He had already been involved in the kidnap and murder of a young member of France's former royal family. Later, he worked as an agent for Napoleon in England and in France. Napoleon paid him handsomely for his services, and Schulmeister became the proud owner of two great estates in France. He himself hoped for an official decoration. His greatest ambition was to be received into the French Legion of Honour. But Napoleon was strict on this point. "Gold," he said, "is the only suitable reward for spies."

Schulmeister lost half his fortune when Napoleon was defeated at Waterloo in 1815. The other half he lost by gambling in stocks and shares. Napoleon's "Emperor of Spies" died in 1853, the impoverished owner of a tobacco kiosk in Strasbourg.

◀ Karl Schulmeister (1770–1853). Napoleon called him "my Emperor of Spies". He came from Alsace and began his career as a smuggler before joining Napoleon's Secret Service.

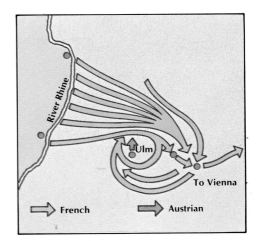

▶ Map of the victory at Ulm. The French army raced from the Rhine frontier to encircle the fortress and capture the Austrian troops. "One spy in the right place is worth 20,000 men in the field," wrote Napoleon.

▲ Marshal Mack surrenders his troops to Napoleon (1805).

After the defeat, the unfortunate Marshal Mack was disgraced and imprisoned as a traitor by the Austrians. He was only released when Schulmeister's real loyalties were revealed, after the French occupied Vienna.

Three Women

The American Civil War

Women often appear in spy stories simply as glamorous bait, used to trap dedicated male agents. The truth is very different. Women have proved just as determined and resourceful as the most successful men. Three women spies of the Civil War fought between the Northern and Southern states of America, were outstanding: Elizabeth Van Lew, Belle Boyd and Rose Greenhow.

The North's most valuable agent was an untrained woman called Elizabeth Van Lew. She lived in Richmond, Virginia, the very heart of the Southern Confederacy. It was well-known that she supported the Northerners in their desire to abolish slavery. In fact, she had long since freed her own black slaves. But she was so loud in her support for the Northern cause that few suspected she could actually be working for them. Her Southern friends thought she was a little mad. They called her "Crazy Bet".

Southern officers searched her house more than once, but they never found evidence of betrayal. Nor did they find the secret room, built under the sloping roof of her house and entered through a door hidden behind a chest of drawers. From here, "Crazy Bet" ran her spy service, and it was here too that she hid Northern agents and escaped prisoners of war until they could be got free. She had a secure route for the information she acquired. It was written in a cipher she invented herself, and passed on through five relay stations before it reached the Northern command.

After the war, General Ulysses Grant told her, "You have sent me the most valuable information received from Richmond during the war." But she had spent a fortune financing her service and the Government never repaid it. She died in poverty, disowned by the people of Virginia for betraying the Southern cause.

The South had its own women spies, however. Belle Boyd was one. She lived in Martinsburg, Virginia, a town which was occupied by Northern troops. Here she gleaned a mass of information. One piece was particularly important. Belle discovered that Northern troops were planning to destroy certain bridges to cut off the route of a Southern column marching to help the Southern General "Stonewall" Jackson. Belle had to run across open fields, shelled and raked with bullets, to carry her message through: but she saved the bridges.

Afterwards, General Jackson wrote in person to Belle: "I thank you for myself and for the army for the immense service that you have rendered your country today." Belle was later imprisoned by the Northerners, but survived the war and later wrote a best-selling book about her career.

The most important single spy "scoop" of the war was the work of another Southern woman spy. She was Rose Greenhow, who operated inside the Northern capital of Washington, with the help of her two couriers Betty Duval and Lillie McKall. In July 1861, she found out that Northern troops were planning to advance on Virginia. She even discovered the route. She passed on the news and as a result the Southerners won the crucial First Battle of Bull Run.

▲ Belle Boyd (an engraving from her book *Belle Boyd in Camp and Prison*). Northern soldiers occupied her home town when she was only 17. When a soldier kicked in the door of her house, Belle Boyd shot him dead.

▼ Rose Greenhow. Returning from a secret mission to England in 1864, her ship was run aground by a Northern gunboat. Rose drowned as she tried to escape.

"SAFE HOUSE"

▼ A "safe house" is a secure hiding place for agents. "Crazy Bet" had a secret room in which she housed escaped Northern soldiers. It was a narrow chamber built between the inside and outside walls of her house, and concealed behind an antique chest of drawers. The only person who ever found out about it was her niece, who stole up one day and saw her aunt standing before "a black hole in the wall" with a platter of food. There in the darkness stood a bearded man in a dirty blue uniform, staring out with haggard eyes.

The girl stole quietly away and never mentioned the incident to her aunt, but she came back later and spoke to the soldier. Aunt Betty had good reason to avoid prying eyes. "What a spanking you would've got," said the soldier, "if your aunt had turned around!"

The secret room was discovered long after the Civil War when "Crazy Bet's" house was being demolished.

Bismarck's Sleuth-hound

Stieber in Prussia and Germany

In 1848 King Frederick Wilhelm of Prussia was being jeered by an angry crowd in Berlin. Their mood was dangerous. Suddenly a man rushed out of the mob and ran towards the king shouting "Death to the tyrant!" When he reached the terrified monarch however, the man dropped his voice and said "Don't be afraid, your Majesty. I am a police agent. My men are in the crowd. They will see that nothing happens to you."

Then he shouted more loud threats and jostled the king to a doorway leading off the street. He pushed the king through and locked the door. Once safe from the mob, the man introduced himself. His name was Wilhelm Stieber.

Stieber was an ambitious young lawyer who also worked undercover as a police spy. The king was so grateful for his escape that two years later he made Stieber Commissioner of Police. Stieber's long career as a spymaster began.

His greatest achievements came in the 1860s. In that period, he helped the Prussian prime minister Bismarck to win two important wars. The first was fought against Austria, the second against France. Stieber's task was to find out about the enemies' strength and readiness for war. He did not just sit back and give orders to his spies. The shady "sleuth-hound" liked to take part in operations himself.

Before the war against Austria, for example, he personally toured the proposed battle zones. Stieber went in disguise. He posed as a travelling salesman with a cartload of cheap religious statuettes. But "under the counter" he also sold things more likely to win the friendship of the bored Austrian soldiers and peasants that he met: pornographic pictures.

Before the French war, Stieber again toured enemy territory. But this time he also sent in literally thousands of spies. They sought out arms dumps and defence works. They reported on the state of French roads, so that Prussian troops would be able to move quickly when they invaded France. They listed the stock of hundreds of French farms, so that the troops would know where to find food. This degree of "penetration" was quite new to espionage. After the Prussian victory, Stieber extended his operations throughout Europe. He employed foreign railway workers, waiters, factory hands and hotel staff. Several German businesses abroad were staffed entirely with his spies. The German Secret Service became the most feared in Europe.

Stieber introduced a policy of "*Schrecklichkeit*" (frightfulness). His spies, he insisted, should kill enemy spies just as soldiers kill each other in wartime. He also compiled files on the private lives of the rich and powerful: these could be useful for blackmail. Stieber died in 1892, and his funeral was well attended by world leaders and nobility. It was said, however, that they did not come to pay their last respects: they came to make sure that the old sleuth-hound was really dead.

▼ **Prince von Bismarck (1815-98).** When he came to power, Prussia was just one of several German states. Bismarck was determined to join the states and build a single united Germany. But first he had to defeat Prussia's enemies, Austria and France. Stieber and his spies gave valuable assistance in the two campaigns.

▲ The Prussians defeat the French in 1871.

▼ Wilhelm Stieber (1818-92). Bismarck called him "my king of sleuth-hounds". Stieber started his career as a criminal lawyer. His contacts in the world of crime were to be useful when he became Germany's first great spymaster.

1. A waiter spies on French soldiers as they talk at a cafe table. 2. A hotel valet opens a customer's suitcase. 3. A railway worker watches the movement of troop trains.

Stieber used thousands of spies to gather information abroad. Every scrap of information might prove valuable.

Inside Germany itself, Stieber kept files on important officials. He set up a special "Green House" in Berlin. This was filled with glamorous women spies. The women trapped their victims in scandalous situations. Then the victims were blackmailed so that they would help Stieber's Secret Service.

Agent Provocateur
Yevno Azeff in Russia

▲ The mysterious Yevno Azeff, bathing with a lady friend. Azeff became an *agent provocateur*, a secret agent who is hired to provoke conspirators into some sort of criminal action, so that they can be arrested.

> *"Yevno Azeff is intelligent and a clever intriguer. He is in close touch with young Jewish students living abroad and he could thus be of real use to us as an agent. It can also be assumed that his greed and his present state of need will make him zealous in his duty . . ."*
> *OCHRANA REPORT, 1893*

▲ Ochrana report on Azeff, filed soon after he got in touch with them.

▶ "Arrest of a revolutionary propagandist", a painting by the great Russian artist Repin.
   The Ochrana (Russian Secret Police) was a vast organization which employed hundreds of spies and *agents provocateurs*. The aim was to stop revolutionaries from overthrowing the Tsar (Russian Emperor). But the Ochrana's plots became so devious that its leaders began to lose track of who was really on their side.

Yevno Azeff was a poor Russian student who was learning engineering at the German Polytechnic of Karlsruhe. There were many other Russians at the school, and several held revolutionary views. On 4 April 1893, Azeff decided to earn a little extra money. He wrote to the Ochrana (the Russian Secret Police), offering to spy on his revolutionary comrades. The Ochrana replied evasively, "We know about the Karlsruhe group and we are not very interested in it. Therefore you are not of such great value to us. Nevertheless, we are prepared to pay you; on condition, however, that you reveal your name." Azeff's extraordinary career as a police spy began soon afterwards.

In the next few months, the quiet Azeff seemed to become a fervent revolutionary. His comrades at Karslruhe were impressed. He began to attend big revolutionary meetings, and joined the newly formed Union of Social Revolutionaries abroad. He posed as a silent man of action, impatient with mere theories and anxious to start terrorist activities inside Russia.

Not everyone was taken in. One revolutionary even accused Azeff publicly of being a spy; but Azeff managed to convince the others of his innocence and the unlucky revolutionary was expelled.

▲ The assassination of Plehve, a bomb plot hatched by Azeff and carried out by the Battle Organization.

Gradually, Azeff moved higher and higher in the revolutionary group. Meanwhile, the Ochrana doubled their payments to him, for his reports were becoming more and more valuable. They decided he should spy on terrorists inside Russia itself.

Azeff came back and secretly betrayed the leader of the terrorist "Battle Organization" to the Ochrana. With their leader arrested, the terrorists were in confusion. Who should take over the leadership but the "man of action" himself, Yevno Azeff.

Azeff now began to run a team of dedicated killers committing terrorist acts against his own masters, whilst receiving huge sums from them in payment. On Azeff's orders, Plehve, the Russian Minister of the Interior, was assassinated in a bomb plot of 1904. A few months later, the Grand Duke Sergei, uncle of the Tsar himself, was killed. Azeff became a revolutionary hero, the supreme expert at assassination.

Why did the Ochrana allow him to go so far? He was their top agent, and perhaps his Ochrana chiefs believed that he needed his grim "successes" if he were to stay at the head of the Battle Organization. Whatever the truth, it was not the Ochrana but the revolutionaries who finally ended Azeff's career. His connections with the Ochrana were discovered. Azeff realised that his cover had been blown, and fled abroad.

Where did his own sympathies lie? The answer remains a mystery. His Ochrana chief later claimed he worked only for money. Perhaps that is the final truth. Yet in 1912, Azeff met a former revolutionary comrade and complained, "If you had not exposed me, I would have killed the Tsar."

Opera Ball

An Austrian Spy

The Austrian Secret Service was thought to be one of the best in the world. It was modernized by a brilliant spymaster called Alfred Redl. He was the Chief from 1907-1911, and he brought in many new methods. Redl was then given a higher post in the army, and his place was taken by another efficient man called Ronge, shortly before World War One.

Ronge was very thorough. As war in Europe seemed more and more likely, he started strict postal censorship (the examination of all suspicious letters).

Two such letters were discovered in March 1913. They were addressed to a post office in Vienna with the code-name "Opera Ball 13" written on them. They had been sent from a town near the Russian border, which made them more suspicious still, for Russia was Austria's enemy. When opened, the letters were found to contain 14,000 kroner (about £900). Could this be payment for a spy?

A secret alarm bell was installed in the post office. Two detectives waited in the police station next door for "Opera Ball" to pick up the letters.

Weeks passed and no-one turned up. The detectives grew bored. On May 14, a man walked into the post office and claimed the letters. Neither detective was at his post. One was in the toilet, and the other was washing his hands. The post office clerk rang his bell and tried to delay the suspect, but by the time the detectives arrived, the suspect had left by taxi, taking the letters with him.

The detectives were appalled. But they learned, when the taxi driver returned, that he had driven the man to a café. They followed anxiously. When they arrived at the café, the suspect had already left. He had taken another taxi to a hotel. Again, the detectives hurried after him.

They did not know what the suspect looked like, but he had dropped the sheath of a pocket knife in one of the taxis. The detectives formed a plan. They told the hotel porter to ask any new arrivals whether they had, by any chance, lost the sheath of a pocket knife. Then they waited in the lobby, pretending to read newspapers.

A middle-aged man came down the stairs. The porter offered him the sheath and he accepted it. At last, the detectives had got their man. But they were shocked and amazed, for they knew him by sight. He was Colonel Alfred Redl, former Chief of the Secret Service!

Was it possible that the great spymaster had been playing a double game? One detective contacted the new Chief, whilst the other shadowed Redl through the streets of Vienna.

Redl must have known that he was being followed and that his game was up, for he returned to the hotel. That night, four officers arrived to arrest him. "I know why you have come," he said.

He asked for permission to write a few words in private. Then, closing the door behind him, he wrote a farewell note and blew out his brains with a revolver.

▲Alfred Redl (died 1913). He was Deputy Chief of the Austrian Secret Service from 1900 to 1905, and Chief from 1907 to 1911.

He was a brilliant spymaster, but he also had a taste for the high life. He ran up large debts. When the Russians offered him money to betray Austrian secrets, he accepted. For ten years, he supplied them with vital information.

> "Levity and passion have destroyed me. Pray for me. I pay with my life for my sins.
>
> *Alfred*
>
> 1.15 a.m. I will die now. Please do not permit a post-mortem examination. Pray for me."

▲Redl's suicide note. He killed himself with a revolver borrowed from one of the officers sent to arrest him. They allowed him to take his life because they did not want the affair made public by putting him on trial. Before he retired to his room, he told them they would find all they needed to know about his spying activities at his house in Prague.

REDL'S ROOM

▼As head of the Secret Service, Redl introduced many new methods. He interviewed suspects in a room filled with devices designed to incriminate his victims: 1. Cigarette case coated with a substance called minium which could be developed to show fingerprints. 2. Recording equipment: the suspect's voice was recorded onto a gramophone disc (there were no tape recorders at this time). 3. Hidden camera. 4. File marked "Geheim" (Secret) also coated with minium. This was left on Redl's desk. He would leave the room, and in his absence some suspects could not resist the temptation to examine it. This gave a clue to their reliability.

THE BETRAYAL OF PLAN A

◀ Serbian soldiers of the period.

Redl's greatest betrayal was to give the Russians a copy of Austria's Plan A. This was a carefully worked out plan for an attack on Serbia. The Russians were friends of the Serbs and passed on the information.

War came so soon after Redl's exposure that the Austrians did not have time to work out a good alternative. They did attack Serbia according to a variation of Plan A. The whole world read of "gallant little Serbia" holding off the mighty Austrian army, but few knew how the Serbs came to be so well prepared.

It has been estimated that Redl's treachery cost the Austrians half a million men in deaths and casualties.

Spies of World War One

1914-1918

Most governments imposed strict postal censorship during World War One. On one occasion, the British censors achieved a great success as a result. They discovered that a newspaper sent from Deptford was addressed to a place in Amsterdam which was on their List of Suspected Addresses. Tests showed that a message had been written on it in invisible ink. The message read simply, "C has gone North. Am sending from 201."

Scotland Yard detectives were informed at once. Since the paper had been sent from Deptford, they checked to see whether there was a street in Deptford long enough to include a "201" address. There was only one, the High Street. The address turned out to be the shop of a baker called Peter Hahn, a man of German origin; and a bottle of invisible ink was found on the premises.

Through Hahn, Scotland Yard were able to trace the mysterious "C". He turned out to be a crack German agent called Müller, who had "gone North" to gain information on British naval bases. Müller was tried and executed. But the British went on sending messages to the Amsterdam address in his name—messages containing false information, of course. They even received £400 payment for the dead agent before the Germans found out that he had been blown.

▲Marthe Richer, a French girl who was employed by the Germans as a secret agent, but was really a loyal patriot. She revealed to the French details of new secret ink capsules used by German Intelligence and also sent details of the new German U-52 submarine.

"STRIPPING"

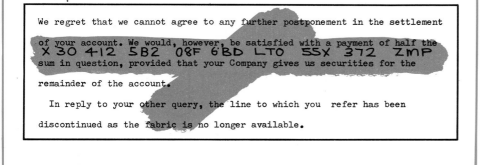

> We regret that we cannot agree to any further postponement in the settlement of your account. We would, however, be satisfied with a payment of half the sum in question, provided that your Company gives us securities for the remainder of the account.
>
> In reply to your other query, the line to which you refer has been discontinued as the fabric is no longer available.

Censors used a process called "stripping" to detect invisible ink. A chemical developer was "stripped" at random across a suspected letter or newspaper. If it picked up a trace of secret writing between the lines, the rest of the message was then developed.

> We regret that we cannot agree to any further postponement in the settlement of your account. We would, however, be satisfied with a payment of half the sum in question, provided that your Company gives us securities for the remainder of the account.
>
> X 30 4-12 5B2 08F 6BD LTO 5SX 372 ZMP
>
> In reply to your other query, the line to which you refer has been discontinued as the fabric is no longer available.

▲ The British Colonel T. E. Lawrence, known as "Lawrence of Arabia." He spoke excellent Arabic and disguised himself as an Arab to roam through Turkish lands in the desert and raise a great revolt against Turkish rule. He died in a motorcycle accident after the war.

Spy scares were rife everywhere. At home, anyone with a foreign sounding name was suspected, and many innocent people suffered as a result. Yet there were plenty of real life spies at work, for espionage was becoming a skilled profession. Training centres and "spy schools" were set up by all the leading nations. The Germans had no less than three spy schools. From their school at Baden-Baden, one promising girl graduate went on to become head of a new spy school set up in Antwerp, in occupied Belgium. Her name was Dr Elsbeth Schragmüller, and she was known as the "Fräulein Doktor". Under her stern leadership, the Antwerp school became the most notorious for its thoroughness.

The professional approach also accounts for the single most important spy scoop of the war. For without the establishment of "Room 40", a special code-breaking department in the British Admiralty, the Zimmermann Telegram might have passed unnoticed: America might not have entered the war.

World War One was a war of great empires, and both sides used secret agents to stir up discontent among local peoples who lived inside enemy territories. The British Colonel T. E. Lawrence worked among Arab tribesmen in the desert empire of Germany's ally, Turkey. In Persia, the German Consul, Wassmuss, worked among the hill tribesmen against the British in much the same way.

The list of great spies is a long one, but few have become more famous than Mata Hari, the exotic dancer executed in 1917. Was she really a spy at all? Some historians have come to doubt it. She was glamorous, mysterious and she had lovers in many countries, but nothing conclusive was ever proved against her.

▲ Mata Hari, "Eye of the Dawn", the exotic dancer who became the most famous female spy in history. Her real name was Margaret Zelle (later Margaret Macleod). She was arrested by the French as a German spy, in 1917. Although she claimed to be innocent, she was executed.

▲ The coded Zimmermann telegram was a secret message sent by the Germans to their Ambassador in Mexico. It proposed that if America joined the war, Germany would offer an alliance to Mexico against America.

The British intercepted the telegram and cipher experts in Room 40 set to work cracking the code. It took several days. They informed the Americans of its contents on 22 February 1917. The Americans were outraged. They declared war on Germany just over a month later.

"Q SHIPS"

▲▼ The British used special ships to counter the threat from German submarines. They were called "Q ships" and looked like innocent merchant ships. If a submarine spotted one, it would rise to the surface to attack. Then the Q ship's false deck houses were removed to reveal guns.

A German spy called Jules Silber passed himself off as a Canadian and got a job as a British Postal Censor. He found out about the Q ships and passed on the news to the German High Command.

Crossing the Lines

1914-1918

Most of the fighting in World War One took place in the trenches. The fortified lines stretched for miles. "Crossing the lines" became the main task of spies in the field.

The most startling development was the use of parachutes to drop spies into enemy territory. It was dangerous work, usually carried out at night. Aviation itself was new to warfare, and parachuting needed special courage.

Parachute spies were often carried in a metal compartment built under the fuselage of an aircraft. The trap-door was operated by the aviator. This crude method made sure that the spy did drop, even if his nerve failed him at the last moment. It also created problems. The Italian parachute spy, Lt Alessandro Tandura, fell asleep in his cramped and stuffy compartment. He awoke falling in pitch darkness about 3,000 metres from the ground. However, he landed safely.

Spies were often dropped into areas where a resident spy ring was already at work. The local spies had to be sure that the new arrivals were on their side, and not enemy agents. The Belgian Marthe Cnockaert ran a big spy ring with an efficient means of identification. Agents sent to help her wore two safety pins fastened under the lapels of their jackets. They were known as "Safety Pin Men" for this reason.

▲ Parachute spies often dropped in uniform, for captured soldiers were usually imprisoned, whilst spies were almost always executed.

Getting information back from behind the lines was difficult. Carrier pigeons were often used to send messages but the birds needed a lot of attention. For example, they had to be fed twice a day. Spies had to carry them with them if they went on long excursions. Some spies cut deep pockets into their waistcoats to conceal their pigeons but the dangers of being found out remained. Later, spies used wireless equipment more often. The transmitter could be left hidden for days without the spy needing to be near it.

Couriers also carried messages across the lines. They developed many cunning ways of concealing them. Some hid messages in the heels of their shoes. One spy hid a message inside a glass eye, while another hid one inside a wooden leg. A Belgian spy ring operated near the border of neutral Holland. When someone died in their area, members of the ring asked the Germans for permission to bury the body in peaceful Dutch ground. Then they sent messages to the British consul in Holland, Major Oppenheim, in the coffin.

Some spies were picked up by plane when their mission was over. But this was dangerous. It was hard to land a plane behind the lines without being spotted. Most spies had to find their own way back. If they were caught, they were almost always shot. People began to question the value of such dangerous missions. Developments in reconnaissance planes and balloons meant that military leaders could now get better results by crossing the lines at several thousand metres above the ground.

▲ Having landed safely, the spy would bury his uniform and parachute pack. His equipment often included a basket of carrier pigeons.

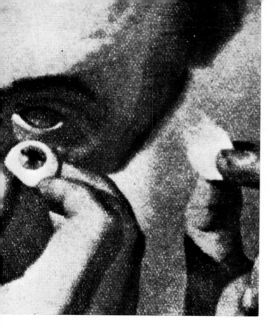

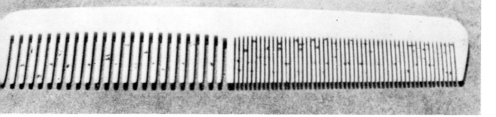

▲Wireless equipment could be hidden inside a cutaway water bottle.

Above left: a spy hides his message inside a glass eye.

◄ A coded message picked out on the teeth of a comb.

▲A field telephone of World War One. Messages could be passed from trench to trench by telephone. But it was easy for spies to tap the lines and listen to conversations. Wise army chiefs would send their messages in code if they used the telephone at all.

◄ A spy operates a secret wireless transmitter. An assistant keeps watch.
  Transmitters were more suitable for sending messages than carrier pigeons. They did not need feeding and could be hidden away for days. But wireless messages could be intercepted so it was vital to transmit in code.

Spies of World War Two

1939-1945

▲ Richard Sorge (1895–1944). In 1965, the Russians issued this four kopeck stamp to commemorate their master spy in the Far East.

Sorge was arrested by the Japanese in 1941 and executed three years later.

▼ A British poster of World War Two warns of danger from spies.

World War Two was more truly a world-wide conflict than World War One. It was also more mobile. Tanks, planes and massive parachute drops allowed armies to move swiftly. Advance information about the enemy's intentions was vital.

In this setting, one spy was outstanding. His name was Richard Sorge, and he had been operating long before the war broke out. Sorge was a German journalist who worked in Japan. He was a great party-goer and got to know many top Japanese officials. His articles also brought him to the attention of leading German Nazis in the Far East, and they often confided in him. They did not know that Sorge was in fact a Communist, spying for Soviet Russia and heading a team of five highly placed agents in Tokyo. From 1935 to his arrest in October 1941, Sorge's ring passed on a continuous stream of top secret information, by courier, and by short-wave radio transmissions to Moscow.

One of Sorge's scoops was to get advance knowledge of Japan's plan to make a sudden attack on America's naval base at Pearl Harbour in the Pacific Ocean. Unfortunately, the Japanese attack took America by surprise.

The Americans later made up for this early defeat with a spy scoop of their own. It was called Operation MAGIC. The Japanese had invented a cipher machine, known as the Purple Encoding Machine. They believed it was foolproof, and throughout the war they sent most of their secret naval commands in the Purple Code. But American cipher experts cracked the code and even built their own model of the Purple Machine. As a result, they could predict Japanese naval movements in advance throughout the Pacific War.

MAGIC was a professional operation, but there was still room for amateurs. The valet of the British ambassador in Turkey offered to spy for the Germans. Code-named "Cicero", he stole and photographed almost every top secret document that passed through the ambassador's hands. Luckily, the Germans believed that the documents were "planted" by the British and failed to take action. After the war, when Cicero tried to use the huge sum of money he had been paid, he was arrested as a forger, for the Germans had paid him in counterfeit notes.

German suspicions were understandable. The British did plan several deception operations. They also set up a special body to train and equip agents for work with the Resistance. The body was called the SOE (Special Operations Executive). Enormous ingenuity was used in designing useful gadgets for its agents. Tiny telescopes were built into cigarette tips, maps were printed on paper so fine that they could be hidden in the shafts of propelling pencils, compasses were fitted into cuff-links. In the cellars below London's Science Museum, a whole department of scientists worked to produce forged identity cards and work permits for each agent's target area.

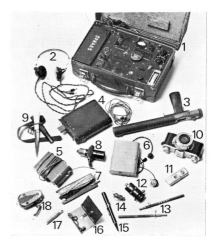

Some tools for spying and sabotage:
1. Radio transceiver (a set which both transmits and receives).
2. Headphones for transceiver.
3. Silent pistol.
4. Radio transmitter.
5. Power pack.
6. Receiver.
7. Aerial
8. Adaptor for transmitter.
9. Indian wrist dagger.
10. Kodak camera (adapted for documents).
11. Rega Minox camera.
12. German igniter.
13. Delayed action detonators.
14. German igniter.
15. Gas pistol pencil.
16. British igniter.
17. Medicine tube (for concealing detonators).
18. Hand-pump torch.

▼ SOE agent in training, using a pram as a shooting stand.

▼ Forged identity card of the SOE heroine Violette Szabo.

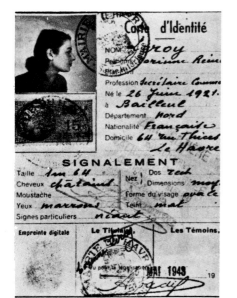

Resistance

1939-1945

▲ A German poster warns of danger from spies.

▼ Weapons training in a French resistance group.

From 1940-45, the Germans were masters of Europe, but inside every occupied country resistance groups carried on the fight. The groups often used short-wave radios to transmit information. The sets were known as "musical boxes" and from the term came the name of a big Communist network which operated inside Germany itself. It was called the "Red Orchestra" and it "played" to Moscow for three years. The Red Orchestra gleaned information from sympathisers inside the German Foreign Office, Air Ministry and Ministries of Labour and Propaganda. The Nazi leaders were furious. When they broke the rings in 1942, they executed eleven leaders in a particularly gruesome way, hanging them by meat-hooks through their throats.

Radio transmission brought special problems. Transmitters could be located by a process known as "triangulation", and if a radio were captured it could be used to transmit false information. The German Intelligence officer, Colonel Giskes, developed this *"Funkspiele"* (radio game) into a fine art. He captured a transmitter which the Dutch resistance used to keep in contact with the British SOE. Giskes then sent messages over the captured transmitter, giving false news of great successes by the resistance in Holland. Send more agents, he insisted. The British did so. Agent after agent was parachuted into Holland, only to be snatched by Giskes' men as soon as they arrived.

▼ Wooden cows set up at a V-2 training ground. To enemy aircraft, the rocket base would look like a field of pasture.

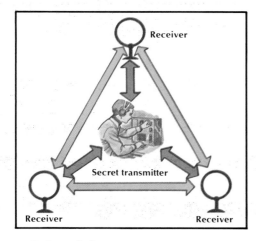

▲ "Triangulation". A radio receiver can detect the direction from which a signal is coming, but not the exact spot. If three receivers surround a signal, however, they can chart the position of the transmitter fairly accurately, by finding the point at which their beams intersect.

Wise operators transmitted from different places, and only transmitted swift, short messages.

▶ Girls of the Dutch resistance take secret photographs. One has a camera concealed in her basket, the other keeps watch.

Not all information was gathered by trained agents and transmitted by radio. Untrained civilians were the backbone of the resistance. Thousands of ordinary men and women lived day in, day out, in constant fear of being found out. They endured the daily threats of torture and execution rather than admit defeat.

A French housepainter called René Duchez was one such man. He got a job working for the German Todt Organization. This was responsible for building a great system of beach defences on the North coast of France. Duchez managed to steal a vital map of this "Atlantic Wall", and the map travelled on its perilous way to London in a sealed biscuit tin, carried by a fishing boat to a British trawler. Knowledge of the Atlantic Wall was to prove critically important to the Allies when they made their D-Day landings.

Resistance groups were active wherever the Germans developed new military projects. One Norwegian group repeatedly sabotaged German attempts to make the "heavy water" necessary for the production of atomic bombs.

Several different groups managed to find the sites of Germany's flying bomb bases. It was an amazing achievement since the Germans had done their utmost to keep the bases secret: at one site, they installed wooden cows to camouflage it from enemy planes. Yet the information got through. A Polish resistance group even captured a V-I flying bomb and smuggled it to England.

Operation Mincemeat

"Major Martin", 1943

The year was 1943. The Allies had captured North Africa and were ready to invade occupied Europe. They decided that Sicily would be the best place to land the troops. But they also realized that the Germans would defend Sicily very heavily. Could the Germans be deceived into thinking that the landings would take place elsewhere? British Intelligence chiefs pondered the problem, and came up with an extraordinary scheme. It was code-named "Operation Mincemeat", and its hero was a corpse.

The Intelligence chiefs obtained the body of a man who had died of pneumonia. They decided to dress the corpse in the uniform of a Royal Marine officer, and give him papers which would indicate that he was a certain "Major Martin", on a secret mission to the Allied leaders in North Africa. "Major Martin" was to carry fake secret documents which hinted that the great invasion would not take place in Sicily, but in Sardinia and Greece.

The body was to be taken in secret by submarine to the coast off Huelva in Spain and slipped into the waves. It was to appear that "Major Martin" had drowned after his plane had crashed at sea. It was known that there were German agents at work in Huelva. They would find out about the body being washed ashore, and report on the documents to the German High Command.

Success depended on how convincing the corpse could be made to look. A whole life had to be invented for the fictitious "Major Martin", and Intelligence officers built his identity with meticulous attention to detail.

▲ "Major Martin's" identity card and the theatre ticket stubs placed in his pocket to suggest he had spent a last night with "Pam". A group of officers actually went to the show.

Getting a photograph for the ID card was a problem. At first, the officers tried photographing the face of the corpse itself, but they could not make it look alive. In the end, they settled for a photograph of someone who looked similar.

◄ "Major Martin" is launched from the submarine *HMS Seraph*. The briefcase full of fake secret documents was strapped to the corpse's wrist to make sure it did not sink. Intelligence officers felt that a real man on a secret mission might well take the same precaution, to ensure that his case was not lost or stolen.

▼ The deception strategy. Sicily was the real invasion target. The aim of "Operation Mincemeat" was to make the Germans believe that the invasion would take place in Greece and Sardinia. The body was dropped off the Spanish coast, for although Spain was neutral, Spanish authorities were friendly with the Germans.

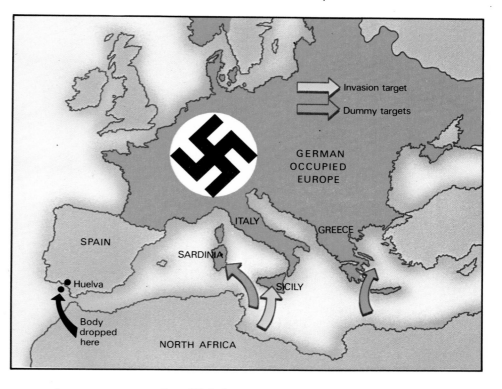

Intelligence officers invented a wartime romance for "Major Martin". A girl in the Admiralty supplied a photograph for him to carry in his wallet, and another forged brilliantly convincing love letters from the supposed girlfriend, "Pam". Love letters are often read many times, and it was important that the fakes should look a bit worn. Of course, they could not just be crumpled up and unfolded. An Intelligence officer carried them around for several days, opening and closing them to give them the right look, before planting them on the body.

Besides the love letters, "Major Martin" carried several other personal documents. There was a bill for an engagement ring, a stern letter from his bank manager, and pompous one from his father. Two theatre ticket stubs were included, to suggest that he had spent a last night out with "Pam" before the fateful "secret mission". As a final touch, Intelligence officers recorded the death of "Major Martin" in the obituary column of *The Times*.

The body was shipped off by submarine inside a large steel canister marked "Optical Instruments". On 30 April 1943, it was removed from the canister and slipped into the waves.

The corpse was recovered in Huelva exactly as planned. German Intelligence papers, recovered after the war, show that the "secret documents" were considered a lucky spy scoop. The Germans sent large detachments of arms and men to Greece and Sardinia, while vital resources were diverted from Sicily. "Operation Mincemeat" was a dramatic success.

> *"The Führer [Hitler] does not agree with the Duce [Mussolini] that the most likely invasion point is Sicily. Furthermore, he believes that the discovered English order confirms the assumption that the planned attack will be directed mainly against Sardinia and Greece."*
>
> *DIARY, ADMIRAL DOENITZ 14 MAY 1943*

▲ According to the diary of the German Admiral Doenitz, the Führer himself (Hitler) was taken in by the hoax. The Duce (Mussolini, leader of Italy) seems to have disagreed.

The Atom Spies

Canada and the United States

▲ Igor Gouzenko, interviewed by a journalist. He wears a hood to protect his identity. After his revelations he lived in fear of Russian reprisals.

During the last years of World War Two, Allied scientists developed the atomic bomb, a devastating weapon capable of destroying whole cities in a single blast. Allied leaders did not want to share their atomic secrets with the Russians, but the Russians were determined to learn them. They built up an extensive network of spy rings in Canada and the United States where the atomic research establishments were set up.

The Allies did not know about the Russian rings until September 1945. Then, only a few days after the Japanese surrender brought the war to an end, a Russian cipher clerk defected. His name was Igor Gouzenko, and he had worked in the Russian embassy in Ottawa, Canada. After Gouzenko's revelations, the round-up of the Canadian network began. One scientist, Klaus Fuchs, was arrested in London in 1949. Like the others, he had worked at the Canadian plant in Chalk River, Ontario. But he had also worked at Los Alamos in America. It was clear that at least one ring was at work there.

Fuchs confessed that he had passed on secrets to a courier who used the name of "Raymond". But he could only remember that "Raymond" was a stocky, round-faced man of middle age. They had met in a number of different American cities as far apart as Santa Fé and New York City. As identification, "Raymond" had carried brown gloves and a book with a green jacket.

"Raymond" was the only lead to the ring. It was vital to trace him. The American FBI (Federal Bureau of Investigation) were faced with a massive task. Where to begin on such slim clues?

First, they checked hotel registers in the towns named as meeting places to find out who had stayed there on the nights of the meetings. They sorted among the thousands of descriptions, weeding out those who could not have been in all the towns on the different dates. Slowly, the lists were reduced.

One of the meetings had taken place in Boston, where Fuchs's sister lived. She came up with a further lead. She remembered the courier discussing chemistry. Her husband remembered another vital clue. Hadn't the man mentioned something about Philadelphia?

The net tightened. Photographs of suspects were flown for identification to Britain, where Fuchs was imprisoned. Yet time and again, the photographs were rejected.

In May 1950, two FBI agents checked up on a certain Harry Gold, a Philadelphia chemist whose name had cropped up on their lists. The quiet little man protested his innocence. For days they questioned him, but always with the same replies. No, he was not a spy. How could he have met Fuchs in all those places? He had never been west of the Mississippi. Then, searching his house, one of the agents discovered a street map of Santa Fé. He confronted Gold. Hadn't he said he had never been west of the Mississippi?

Suddenly, Gold broke down and confessed. Yes, he was "Raymond". His confessions led to the exposure of the big American spy ring.

▲ Rudolf Abel, one Russian master spy who escaped the round-up of the atom spy rings. He kept on operating and was not arrested until 1957.

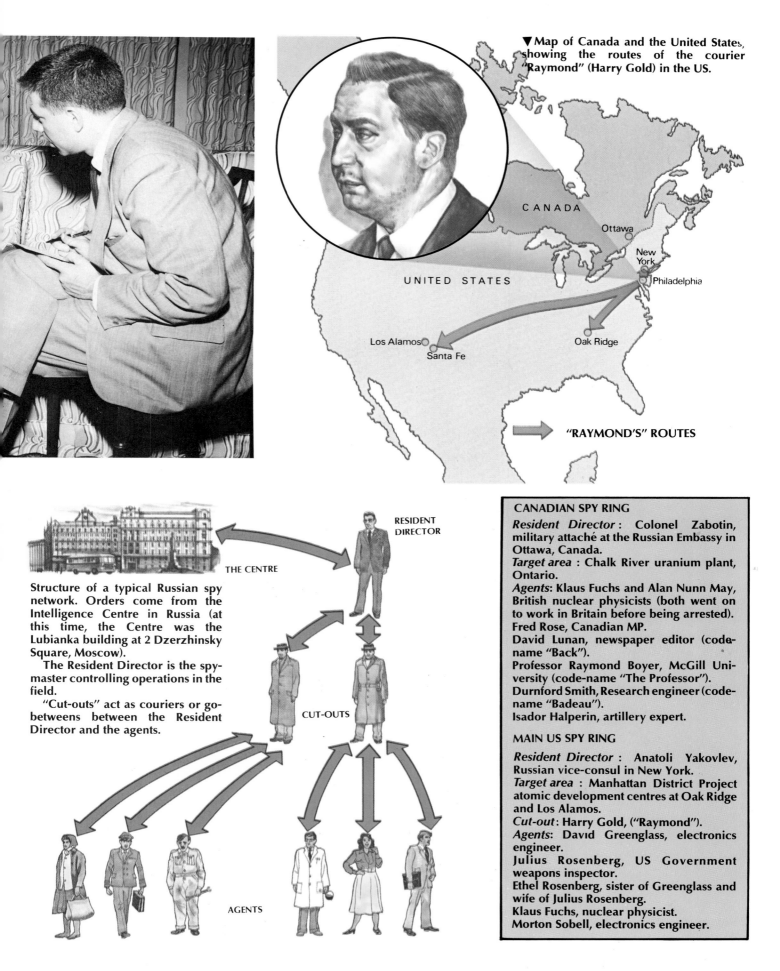

▼Map of Canada and the United States, showing the routes of the courier "Raymond" (Harry Gold) in the US.

CANADA

Ottawa

New York

Philadelphia

UNITED STATES

Los Alamos

Santa Fe

Oak Ridge

"RAYMOND'S" ROUTES

RESIDENT DIRECTOR

THE CENTRE

CUT-OUTS

AGENTS

Structure of a typical Russian spy network. Orders come from the Intelligence Centre in Russia (at this time, the Centre was the Lubianka building at 2 Dzerzhinsky Square, Moscow).

The Resident Director is the spymaster controlling operations in the field.

"Cut-outs" act as couriers or go-betweens between the Resident Director and the agents.

CANADIAN SPY RING

Resident Director : Colonel Zabotin, military attaché at the Russian Embassy in Ottawa, Canada.
Target area : Chalk River uranium plant, Ontario.
Agents: Klaus Fuchs and Alan Nunn May, British nuclear physicists (both went on to work in Britain before being arrested). Fred Rose, Canadian MP.
David Lunan, newspaper editor (code-name "Back").
Professor Raymond Boyer, McGill University (code-name "The Professor").
Durnford Smith, Research engineer (code-name "Badeau").
Isador Halperin, artillery expert.

MAIN US SPY RING

Resident Director : Anatoli Yakovlev, Russian vice-consul in New York.
Target area : Manhattan District Project atomic development centres at Oak Ridge and Los Alamos.
Cut-out: Harry Gold, ("Raymond").
Agents: David Greenglass, electronics engineer.
Julius Rosenberg, US Government weapons inspector.
Ethel Rosenberg, sister of Greenglass and wife of Julius Rosenberg.
Klaus Fuchs, nuclear physicist.
Morton Sobell, electronics engineer.

Spies for Sale

Post-war Germany

At the end of World War Two, the Allies divided Germany in two. The Communist Russians ruled in the East. The British, French and Americans ruled in the West. A new conflict began. It was called the "Cold War" but there was no real fighting between the armies of East and West. The Cold War was fought in diplomacy and espionage. West Germany's ruined cities were breeding grounds for spies. Some were just cheap gangsters, like the "Hundred Mark Boys" who roamed into the East and came back with scraps of information to sell. But there were others with more to offer. One of these was Reinhart Gehlen.

During the war, Gehlen had been one of Hitler's top Intelligence officers. He specialized in spying against Russia and Eastern Europe. While the Allies rounded up leading Nazis for trial after the war, Gehlen kept his head. He told his spies in the East to stay in place and he collected several containers of his valuable files. When the Americans caught up with him, he stayed calm. He had something to offer them in exchange for his freedom. He had his spies and his files to sell.

The Americans accepted the deal. Gehlen was flown in secret to Washington D.C. for the Americans did not want this valuable spymaster to fall into Russian hands. When Gehlen returned in 1946, it was with American backing to set up his own private spy service. He soon began to show his worth. Over the next ten years, the newly formed CIA poured $200 million into the secret Gehlen Organization.

▲ **Reinhart Gehlen (1902-). In 1956, his secret organization became the official Intelligence service of West Germany. Gehlen was its President. He did not retire until 1968. His last years as head were surrounded by scandals about his wartime past and the spies he employed. Two of his officers turned out to be double agents.**

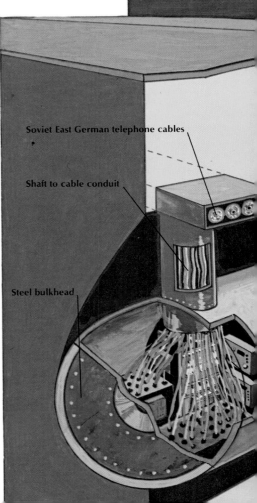

Soviet East German telephone cables

Shaft to cable conduit

Steel bulkhead

▲▲ **A radio operator at Gehlen's secret base at Pullach. Armed guards, posing as "gamekeepers" patrolled the grounds of Pullach in the early days. From here, he kept in** touch with his thousands of "V-men" (trusted agents) in the Communist East. Some were issued with transmitters concealed inside thermos flasks.

The Gehlen Organization operated from Pullach, a former SS housing estate near Munich. It became a fortified centre for espionage. Gehlen also set up fake business companies. One, for example, produced venetian blinds; but in the back rooms, spies were recruited into the widening network.

The CIA and the Gehlen Organization undertook many operations together. The most spectacular was the Telephone Tunnel. In 1955, the Americans were building a new radar station in the suburb of Rudow in West Berlin. CIA agents, with help from Gehlen's experts, used the opportunity to dig a tunnel 600 metres long. It passed under a barbed wire fence right into East Germany. The aim: to tap the main East German telephone lines. It was an amazing feat. Thousands of tons of earth were hauled out on a narrow gauge railway and driven away in covered US army trucks. The sections of the tunnel were welded together underground. Its walls were crammed with recording and amplifying equipment. The switchboard at the end could monitor 432 separate conversations at the same time.

The tunnel was in operation for nine months. But on April 22 1956, the Russians suddenly burst in at the far end. The electric alarm system did its job. The Russians found the tunnel deserted, though all the equipment was still in place. The operators had left so quickly that the Russians found a coffee percolator still bubbling in a deserted chamber.

▲George Blake. He was a Communist double agent inside the British Intelligence Service in Berlin. He is believed to have betrayed the tunnel to the Russians.

In 1961, Blake was exposed as a spy and sentenced to 42 years' imprisonment. But he managed to escape prison and fled to Russia where he still lives today.

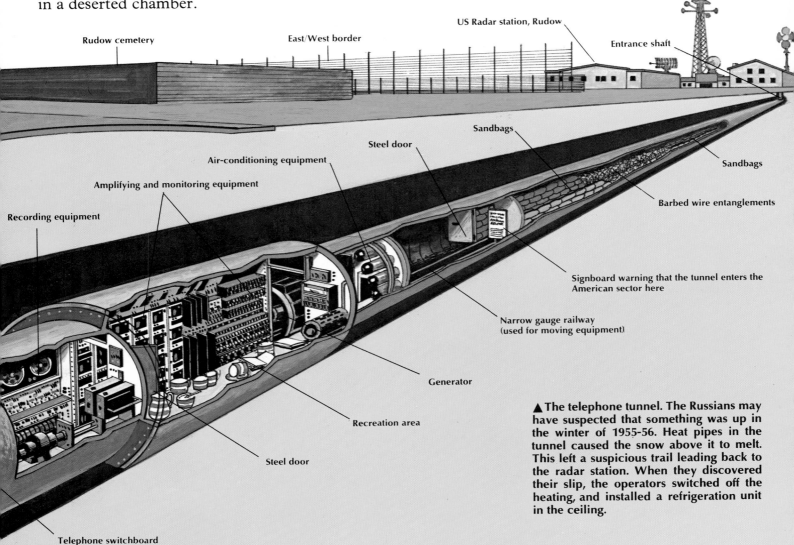

▲The telephone tunnel. The Russians may have suspected that something was up in the winter of 1955-56. Heat pipes in the tunnel caused the snow above it to melt. This left a suspicious trail leading back to the radar station. When they discovered their slip, the operators switched off the heating, and installed a refrigeration unit in the ceiling.

41

Illegals
The Portland Spy Ring

▲ "Gordon Lonsdale" (real name Colonel Konon Molody), a trained "illegal". The Russians got hold of the real birth certificate of a Canadian called Lonsdale who had died in boyhood. Having arrived in Canada, Molody used the certificate to get legitimate passport and identity cards from the Canadian Government. He did not need forged papers.

▲ "Peter and Helen Kroger" (real names Morris and Lona Cohen), trained "illegals". They had worked for Rudolf Abel's spy ring in the United States, and escaped to England when his ring was broken up.

Lonsdale was sentenced to 25 years, the Krogers to 20 years each, and Houghton and Gee to 15 years each.

Early in 1960, security officers at Britain's secret Underwater Weapons Establishment at Portland began to investigate one of their clerks. His name was Harry Houghton and he had been under suspicion before. Now he was buying large rounds of drinks at a local pub, had bought a cottage and a brand new car. How could he afford these luxuries? He was spending more on drink alone than he received in salary. For nine months, MI 5 (British security and counter-espionage) kept Houghton under close watch. They also watched his mistress, Ethel Gee, who worked at Portland too. They discovered that the pair made frequent trips to London, and there met a man called Gordon Lonsdale. At these meetings, Houghton and Lonsdale would hand each other a package. It was not hard to guess what was going on. Houghton and Gee were exchanging secrets for cash. They were small-time spies. But Lonsdale?

On the face of it, Gordon Lonsdale was a successful Canadian businessman. He had lived in Britain for five years, a respected company director who was very popular with women. Nothing in his behaviour suggested the truth. "Gordon Lonsdale" was really a dedicated Russian agent, whose real name was Colonel Konon Trofimovitch Molody. Molody was an "illegal", a trained agent who lives and works under a false name. He had slipped into Canada in 1954 and spent a year there perfecting his accent and obtaining a passport and other identity papers before coming to Britain. His new identity was so convincing, that when he first approached Houghton and Gee, they believed he was an *American* agent, doing a little friendly spying on the Portland Establishment.

On 7 January 1961, Houghton, Gee and Lonsdale were picked up during an exchange of parcels in a dramatic arrest near the *Old Vic* theatre in London. Back at Scotland Yard, Houghton admitted "I've been a bloody fool." Miss Gee tried to pretend she was innocent. But Lonsdale, the professional, maintained complete silence.

Checking up on Lonsdale's friends, however, Superintendent Smith of Scotland Yard decided to pay a visit to the quiet suburban home of Peter and Helen Kroger. They were dealers in rare books, Canadians like Lonsdale, and Lonsdale had made frequent trips to their house at 45 Cranley Drive in Ruislip. They seemed a quiet, friendly couple, and it was hard to believe they knew Lonsdale's real profession. The pair were asked to accompany Superintendent Smith to Scotland Yard for further questioning. Mrs Kroger politely agreed, and she asked whether she could stoke the boiler before leaving the house. "Certainly," replied the Superintendent, "but first let me see what you have got in your handbag." Mrs Kroger refused. The bag was wrested from her and found to contain a six page letter in Russian, three microdots and a typed sheet of code.

The Krogers, like Lonsdale, were "illegals". Their suburban home was found to be packed full of advanced espionage equipment. From Cranley Drive, they had sent Lonsdale's secrets, through coded microdots and radio transmission, to the Centre in Moscow.

45 CRANLEY DRIVE

▼ 45 Cranley Drive. The bathroom was convertible into a photographic darkroom. Forged passports were found in the attic. One radio transmitter was found concealed in a cavity under the kitchen floorboards. Another was found in 1977, long after the Krogers' arrest. The new occupants of the house were digging in the garden one day and dug up the second transmitter.

▲ The Krogers' suburban home was an advanced centre for espionage. A bottle of talcum powder was found on the premises. It had a swivel top, which revealed side compartments for concealing a microfilm viewer.

▼ A cigarette lighter had a false bottom containing signal plans for radio transmission times and frequencies. A similar device was found at Lonsdale's apartment.

▼ The microdots found in Mrs Kroger's handbag, and (right) one of the microdots blown up. This message was a letter which Lonsdale had written to his wife in Moscow.

▲ In the back of a radiogram there was a concealed tape recorder and a wire leading to a trap door in the kitchen floor. The wire led down to the cavity under the floorboards to the hidden radio transmitter.

Agents in Place

Philby and Penkovsky

◄ Kim Philby protests his innocence to newsmen in 1955. Philby, Burgess and Maclean were all at Cambridge University together, where they became Communists. All three were recruited as Communist spies shortly afterwards: we still do not know by whom.

Philby was to be a "sleeper", that is, he should not be active until he had reached a position in which he could be of real value.

Throughout World War Two, he worked his way up in the British Secret Service. Incredibly, he became head of the department dealing with the Russian Intelligence Service.

▼ Kim Philby photographed recently in Russia. The picture was taken by his son. The "Philby Affair" raises inevitable questions. Why was he allowed to operate after Burgess and Maclean defected? Were British Intelligence really deceived by him? Or did they hope he would give himself, and others, away if he were left free?

On 25 May, 1951, British security officers prepared their case against Donald Maclean, a top diplomat suspected of spying for the Russians. The 25th was a Friday, and it was decided to wait until the following Monday before arresting him. That night, Maclean disappeared. So did Guy Burgess, another important diplomat. It was clear that the men had defected to Russia. Worse still, someone high in British Intelligence must have tipped them off. It became vital to find the "third man".

Suspicion fell on Harold "Kim" Philby, a leading British officer of MI 6 (British Intelligence). Philby was questioned for several months, and although nothing was proved against him he was forced to resign. In 1955, an MP named Philby in Parliament as the "third man". Newspapers got hold of the story and Philby was questioned by journalists from all the main British newspapers. Yet throughout his public and private trials, Philby maintained that he was innocent.

There were many old colleagues in MI 6 who felt that Philby had been badly treated. Some thought he had been brought down by rivals in MI 5. In 1956, he was sent to Beirut as a journalist for *The Observer*: and also, it is believed, to work undercover for MI 6. After five years working in Beirut, Philby suddenly disappeared. Soon afterwards, it was announced that he had defected to Russia. He was back, in his own words, "safe and sound". For Philby was indeed the "third man". He had been a Communist agent for 30 years.

▲ Checkpoint Heerstrasse, Berlin, at dawn, 22 April 1964. Here, Greville Wynne was exchanged for the Russian spy "Gordon Lonsdale". The British group are moving to the cars on the right, the Russians to the yellow car on the left.

One day in September 1961, the year of Philby's defection, a smart Russian man strolled along a Moscow boulevard and paused by a sandbox where some children were playing. He smiled and offered one of them a box of sweets. When the man had gone, the child took the box back to the mother who was sitting on a bench nearby. The mother was the wife of a British diplomat in the Moscow Embassy. The box contained four rolls of film of top secret Russian Intelligence documents. And the man was Colonel Oleg Penkovsky, an officer of the GRU (Russian Military Intelligence).

Penkovsky was a spy for the West. His main contact was a British businessman called Greville Wynne, whose work often took him to Moscow. Through Wynne, British and American Intelligence officers supplied Penkovsky with money, a miniature Minox camera and a radio receiver. In 18 months, Penkovsky managed to hand over about 5,000 film exposures of military and Intelligence documents. The film was passed on through "live" contact, as in the method described above, as well as through a number of ingenious "dead letter-boxes".

In October 1962, while Penkovsky was planning to escape to the West for good, he was arrested in Moscow. Wynne was kidnapped in Hungary and brought back to Russia as well. The men were tried and found guilty. Penkovsky was sentenced to death, and Wynne to eight years in prison, but Wynne never served his full term. In 1964, he was exchanged for the Russian spy, "Gordon Lonsdale".

▲ Colonel Oleg Penkovsky of the GRU (Russian Military Intelligence) at his trial. He was sentenced to death and reported to have been executed, but some people claim he is still alive, kept prisoner somewhere in Russia.

At the trial, the Russians produced tape recordings of incriminating conversations between Wynne and Penkovsky. They had been under surveillance for some time before they were arrested.

Spy Schools
Reference

Wartime training

It became clear during the two world wars that proper training centres were needed to teach the basic techniques of espionage and sabotage to agents. The courses at these centres included training in armed and unarmed combat, parachute drops, the use of explosives, radio communication and codes and ciphers.

Great attention was also paid to the routine "do's and don'ts" of spycraft; how to set up dead letter boxes, memorize information and behave without attracting suspicion, for example. Here is a brief extract from advice given to students by Elsbeth Schragmüller, the "Fräulein Doktor" of the German school at Antwerp: "Conceal whatever linguistic gifts you have, to encourage others to speak more freely in your hearing; and remember, no German agent speaks or writes a word of German while on duty abroad . . .

"Do not burn a letter or other paper and treat the charred or ashen fragments as unreadable. Microscopic examination can do a great deal with paper ash. Tearing up papers and throwing them away does not destroy them. Paper scraps are never disposed of with absolute secrecy, even in public lavatories . . ."

"The Farm"

The training school of the American CIA is a huge complex of buildings in Langley, Virginia, known to agents as "the farm". New recruits have to submit to a polygraph (lie detector) test, and their whole family background is carefully examined by security officers before they are accepted.

Courses at "the Farm" stress above all else the importance of security in undercover work. Trainees learn about "bag jobs" (breaking and entering), and bugging. There are also exercises in illegal border crossings carried out at fake borders with control towers.

Endurance tests

In his book "The Man from Moscow", the British businessman, Greville Wynne, describes how he was given a refresher course in espionage by British Intelligence (Wynne had been a wartime agent). The course included a grim endurance test involving several beatings-up: "I went down again, but this time with a punch between the shoulder blades and a slap in the liver. These men were experts, they knew how to hurt without leaving marks."

▼ Greville Wynne describes his refresher course in espionage given by British Intelligence (from his book "The Man from Moscow", Hutchinson & Co. Ltd, 1967).

▲ A "polygraph", or lie detector test. The coil around the subject's chest registers changes which occur in breathing patterns when he tells a lie.

The band around his arm registers changes in pulse rate. The changes are recorded into a sensitive device which charts them on graph paper.

"My training went on at full pressure. I had courses to attend in coding, tape-recording and communications, and a continual insistence on the basic principles which I had learned during the war. Such as:

Observing the physical characteristics of people I met.

When meeting a colleague in public, always to shield the lips with a hand or glass to prevent any lip-reading by a stranger . . .

When passing messages, never do so at arm's length, but always close to the other person.

For a rendez-vous, always to inspect the area beforehand, and never to arrive early or late. If the contact is missing, never to hang about . . .

To choose the sites for dead-letter boxes in places where the picker-up could be seen without suspicion, such as grave-yards, or the entrance halls of buildings, and to vary the sites frequently."

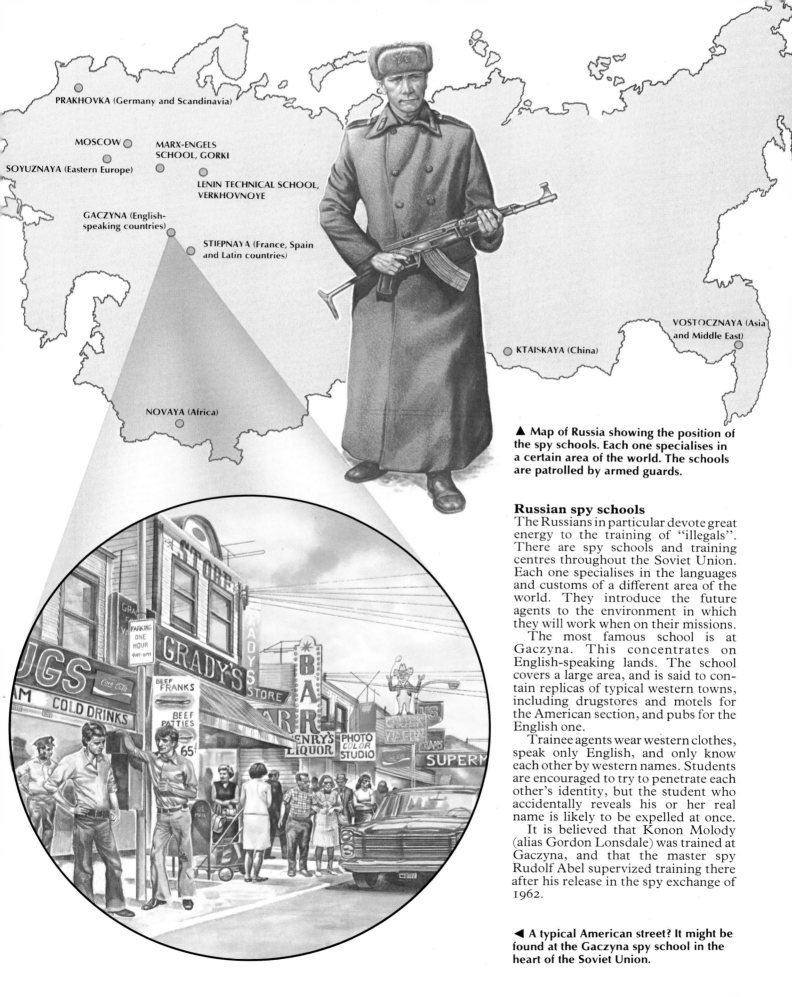

PRAKHOVKA (Germany and Scandinavia)

MOSCOW

MARX-ENGELS
SCHOOL, GORKI

SOYUZNAYA (Eastern Europe)

LENIN TECHNICAL SCHOOL,
VERKHOVNOYE

GACZYNA (English-
speaking countries)

STIEPNAYA (France, Spain
and Latin countries)

VOSTOCZNAYA (Asia
and Middle East)

KTAISKAYA (China)

NOVAYA (Africa)

▲ Map of Russia showing the position of the spy schools. Each one specialises in a certain area of the world. The schools are patrolled by armed guards.

Russian spy schools

The Russians in particular devote great energy to the training of "illegals". There are spy schools and training centres throughout the Soviet Union. Each one specialises in the languages and customs of a different area of the world. They introduce the future agents to the environment in which they will work when on their missions.

The most famous school is at Gaczyna. This concentrates on English-speaking lands. The school covers a large area, and is said to contain replicas of typical western towns, including drugstores and motels for the American section, and pubs for the English one.

Trainee agents wear western clothes, speak only English, and only know each other by western names. Students are encouraged to try to penetrate each other's identity, but the student who accidentally reveals his or her real name is likely to be expelled at once.

It is believed that Konon Molody (alias Gordon Lonsdale) was trained at Gaczyna, and that the master spy Rudolf Abel supervized training there after his release in the spy exchange of 1962.

◀ A typical American street? It might be found at the Gaczyna spy school in the heart of the Soviet Union.

Microspying

Reference

▲ A spy photographs a secret document.

▲ The photograph is photographed again.

MAKING A MICRODOT

MIDDLE (OF) DECEMBER AIRPLANE PARTS AND MA-CHINERY FROM DOUGLAS AND LOCKHEED IN NEW ORLEANS AND GALVESTON ARE TO BE SHIPPED FOR CASABLANCA AND RABAT. THE NAMED FIRMS INTEND TO BUILD THERE ONE ASSEMBLY PLANT EACH IN ORDER TO TAKE UP LATER TOTAL PRODUCTION BY MAKING USE OF AFRICA'S RAW MATERIALS. THE SHIPMENT WILL TAKE PLACE ON FORMER DELTA LINERS. THREE HUNDRED TECHNICIANS OF EACH FIRM ARE GOING ALONG. THE SHIPS WILL BE AT-TACHED TO CONVOY. TECHNICAL VANGUARD HAS ALREADY DEPARTED BY WAY OF PAN-AMERICAN AIRLINES. (I) REPEAT THE NAMES: NEW ORLEANS, GALVESTON, DOUGLAS, LOCKHEED, CASABLANCA, RABAT.

▲ Each time the photograph is shot, its size is reduced. The last photograph is taken through a reversed microscope. Equipment has been produced to simplify this process but spies in the field still use this method quite often.

▲ The dot is handled with a syringe . . .

▲ . . . and fixed to the page of a book.

Miniaturization

Miniature equipment has obvious advantages in espionage, for it can be easily concealed. Today, "micro-spying" is practised not only in military and political espionage, but also in the widening field of "industrial espionage" (spying carried out by business firms on their rivals). Much miniature equipment can be bought freely in shops, and this has created problems. "Bugs" are now banned in many countries, but miniature cameras and radios can still be obtained quite easily.

Microdots

Microdots are tiny pieces of film. They are so small that all of the words on this page could be fitted on to a microdot no bigger than the full stop at the end of this sentence.

German photographic experts developed the modern method of producing microdots in World War Two. A typed message is photographed to reduce the size. The reduced photograph is then photographed again, further reducing the size, and so on. The final shot is taken through a reversed microscope.

The tiny dots are usually handled with a hypodermic syringe. The fine needle is cut away at the end to leave a circle for the dot. Pressure on the plunger will release it, suction will hold it. The dot can then be fixed with adhesive to almost any surface for concealment: the page of an ordinary book, for example.

Cameras and radios

The display window of your high street camera shop may well include a couple of miniature cameras. The smallest can be fitted into a cigarette packet, or even a cigarette lighter. Oleg Penkovsky used a 16mm Minox. An RAF technician called Douglas Britten was issued by the Russians with a flat camera the size of a wallet which could operate in total darkness.

Portable transistor radios became available in the shops after World War Two. They could be made much smaller than the old, bulky valve sets. Espionage technicians were quick to take advantage. Some of Gehlen's "V-men" went into Eastern Europe equipped with tiny transmitters concealed in the tops of thermos flasks. The range of such radios is seldom more than a couple of kilometres.

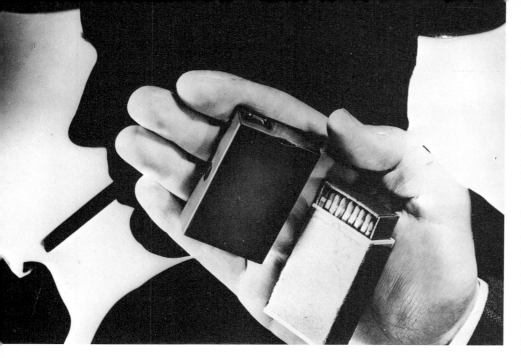

▲ A miniature camera, the size of a box of matches. Its advantages for taking secret photographs are obvious.

▶ This ring belonged to a man who was found drugged and bound inside a trunk at Rome Airport in 1960. It contained a cavity used for storing microfilm.

▼ A bug the size of a shirt button can be concealed behind a tie, and transmit conversation over a distance of 100 metres.

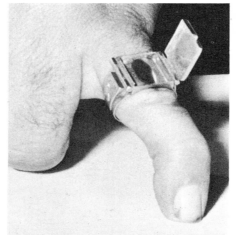

▶ A miniature radio transmitter and receiver. The problem with such tiny radios is that their range is limited.

Bugs and bugging

"Bugs" are electronic listening devices which transmit sound waves to a receiver. Even the smallest bugs may have a range of as much as 50 metres. Bugs can be carried by a mobile agent, or permanently installed in walls or furniture. The problem with permanent bugs is that they may have to be installed by criminal means, such as breaking and entering. The recent Watergate case in America showed the dangers. President Nixon was forced to resign because some men on his staff were found to be involved in an attempt to bug the headquarters of the Democratic party during an election campaign.

Concealed bugs can be detected by counter-espionage technicians. They use devices, similar to geiger counters, which sweep an area and indicate by a series of clicks whether they are close to a bugging device. Today, embassies are regularly swept for bugs as are the board rooms of some top business firms where new products are discussed.

Another device, the "bug eliminator", is used to produce an electronic noise which puts bugs out of action. As a final resort, some embassies have installed special "bug-free" chambers where secret discussions can be held without fear of hidden devices.

Bugging has been used in recent warfare. In Vietnam, the Americans tested out a new system called CASM (Computer-controlled Area Sterilization Multi-sensor System). Hundreds of tiny bugging devices were dropped by aircraft over a certain area to pick up troop and weapon movements in the jungle.

Security and Surveillance

Reference

Security services

Security services aim at preventing important information, and important people, from falling into the hands of the opposition. For example, they try to make sure that spies do not penetrate secret research establishments or government departments. If information does leak out, security services are brought in to investigate. They also protect important officials from assassination.

Prevention is better than cure. Much security work is involved in watching out for anyone who might be a threat in the future. Security services compile files on everybody who occupies an important place in society, as well as on potential trouble-makers. The files may include details of people's private lives, their friends, relations and associates. Modern methods of surveillance are very advanced, and the computer-controlled file rooms of a big security service are vast.

This raises important questions. Does not everyone have a right to lead his or her own private life? Who should decide on what is a threat to security?

In some countries, the whole population is kept under surveillance. People may be imprisoned for things which *we* would not consider dangerous: the right to criticize their leaders freely, for example, or to read whatever books they choose.

Of course, it is important for governments to protect the public from dangerous and irresponsible people. But how can we be sure that government leaders and security services will act responsibly themselves? The Watergate scandal in America posed this problem dramatically.

Surveillance

Surveillance means keeping watch. Security services may keep watch on suspects using some of the "microspying" devices described on pages 48-9. A suspect's telephone may be bugged in a variety of ways, for example. One common method is to use a bug shaped exactly like an ordinary telephone mouthpiece.

Microphones and night viewers

Long-range microphones can be aimed at a sound source from a distance of several hundred metres. They were originally used by naturalists making wild-life recordings. Known as "shotgun" microphones, they are efficient in good conditions, but they are bulky and only really suitable for listening in on conversations held in the open air.

For listening in on conversations held inside a walled room, the most advanced device uses laser beams which are trained at a window and pick up speech vibrations in the glass.

Telescopes and binoculars have long been valuable tools for the spy, but the latest development in long distance viewing is a recent invention: the night vision device for viewing in complete darkness. Early models were infra-red devices and their range was limited to about 250 metres. More recent inventions like the *Startron* have a greater range.

▼ A telephone bug (arrowed). It is hard to detect because it is shaped like a mouthpiece and only activated when the telephone is in use. Below: a "bug detector"

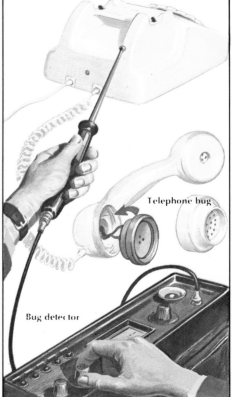

Telephone bug

Bug detector

▲ Under surveillance: a German spy of World War Two has confidential discussions with his lawyer. Secret listening devices pick up their conversation, whilst a concealed camera photographs the event. This episode took place in the United States, and was handled by the FBI.

Tailing a suspect

Suspects are often kept under surveillance for months, or even years. It is better to find a whole spy network by patiently following an agent's movements, than to arrest a single spy. The staff of foreign embassies are sometimes "tailed" on a random basis for a few weeks to see whether they act suspiciously. It is a long job, requiring constant alertness and considerable skill, for the "tail" should never allow the suspect to spot him. It is rare for a single security man to be put on a suspect, for there are several simple ways of throwing off a tail.

A simple method is to take a taxi and direct it down a one way street. If a "tailing vehicle" is following, the suspect can get out, turn a corner and take some other form of transport, leaving the tailing vehicle trapped in the one way system. If there is a "tail" following on foot, the suspect still has plenty of alternatives. The method often used in thrillers is actually common practice: getting on a tube train and then jumping off just as the doors close. A team of four or five men is needed for a really efficient tailing job.

One modern method of tailing a vehicle is to install a tiny "bleep button". This is a small device which emits a radio signal. Wherever the vehicle goes, its movements can be tracked on a radar screen. Of course, this method is of limited value if the suspect decides to leave the vehicle.

DIRECTIONAL MICROPHONE

▲ A parabolic directional microphone for listening from long range. It is sometimes used with the *Startron*. It has a range of up to one kilometre.

▼ *Startron* passive night vision device for viewing over long distances. Such devices are used for watching wildlife as well as for surveillance.

▲ A German security officer photographs a student demonstration to obtain pictures of possible trouble-makers.

NIGHT VISION DEVICE

Weapons of Secret War

Reference

Wartime weapons

During World War Two, Resistance fighters and SOE agents were supplied with a variety of cunningly designed secret weapons. These included silent pistols and gas-pistols disguised as pencils. One favourite SOE weapon was a pen and pencil which, when joined, formed an explosive device.

The weapons had to be small and easy to conceal. For this reason, the standard British Sten gun was often used by Resistance fighters. It was not perfect: it sometimes jammed, for example. But it could be dismantled into pieces small enough to be hidden in a large handbag.

SMERSH

During the war, the Russians formed special units attached to the Red Army. Their aim was to prevent subversion and desertion in the ranks. The units' motto was *Smiert Shpionam* (Death to Spies). The motto was shortened to *SMERSH*. In modern spy thrillers, writers sometimes refer to a deadly organization called SMERSH, but in fact, the SMERSH units were disbanded after the war.

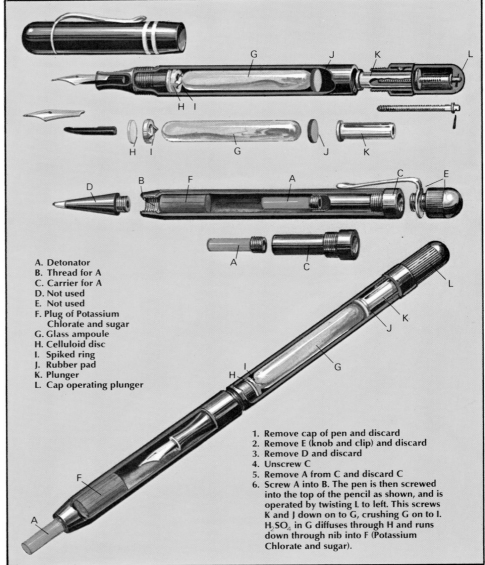

A. Detonator
B. Thread for A
C. Carrier for A
D. Not used
E. Not used
F. Plug of Potassium Chlorate and sugar
G. Glass ampoule
H. Celluloid disc
I. Spiked ring
J. Rubber pad
K. Plunger
L. Cap operating plunger

1. Remove cap of pen and discard
2. Remove E (knob and clip) and discard
3. Remove D and discard
4. Unscrew C
5. Remove A from C and discard C
6. Screw A into B. The pen is then screwed into the top of the pencil as shown, and is operated by twisting L to left. This screws K and J down on to G, crushing G on to I. H_2SO_4 in G diffuses through H and runs down through nib into F (Potassium Chlorate and sugar).

▲ The explosive pen and pencil set issued by the British SOE during World War Two.

1. **Barrel unit**
2. **Trigger unit**
3. **Shoulder stock**
4. **Magazine.**

◄ The Sten Gun could be taken apart. The individual pieces could be carried in a large handbag.

Assassins

The Russian spy service is called the KGB. It contains a special department for carrying out sabotage and assassinations abroad.

In 1954 a Russian agent, Captain Nicolai Khokhlov, defected to the West while on an assassination mission. He produced the weapon he had been supplied with. It was a dummy cigarette case containing a gun which fired bullets of poisonous potassium cyanide.

Seven years later, another Russian killer defected. His name was Bogdan Stashinsky. He admitted to having murdered two men with a special gas gun. This fired capsules of poisonous prussic acid. The vapour was sprayed in the faces of his victims and killed them by paralysing the heart. The gas then dispersed without a trace, giving the impression that the victims had died of heart attacks. To avoid being overcome by the vapour himself, Stashinsky had to take special capsules before and after firing.

Black Operations

The American CIA has also been involved in several sinister operations. These are known in the spy trade as Black Operations or "dirty tricks."

The most famous of these happened in 1961. The CIA trained 1500 Cuban exiles and sent them home to raise a rebellion against the Communist government of Cuba. The expedition was a humiliating defeat for the CIA. The landing at the Bay of Pigs was a disaster. Worse, some of the men who survived used their training to set up as gangsters and racketeers inside the United States itself.

▲Khokhlov's dummy cigarette case. It fired poisonous bullets. The gun was powered by small batteries and fired almost silently.

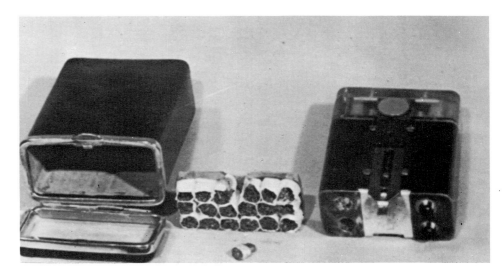

▲The Communist spy Jack Soblen swallowed this handful of nuts and bolts in an attempt to take his own life.

Interrogation

Captured spies run the risk of being tortured for information. They may also be treated with "truth drugs" to reveal their secrets. German Intelligence often used the drug Scopolomine to extract information during World War Two. Other truth drugs include Sodium pentathol, which is known as Soap in spy jargon.

In the last resort, suicide may be the only way for a spy to prevent himself breaking down and giving away secret information. Spies are often issued with poison capsules for use if they are captured.

Gary Powers (see page 56) was issued with a silver dollar containing a poisoned needle, though he did not use it. In America, the Communist spy Jack Soblen was not so well-equipped. In an attempt to take his own life, he swallowed a handful of nuts and bolts, some of them several centimetres long.

Codes and Ciphers

Reference

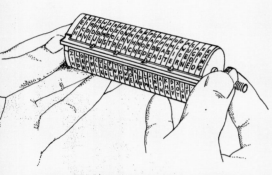

▲ Cipher discs of the 16th century. The inner wheel revolves to give 24 possible cipher alphabets (A could be set at y, or q, or l, etc).

▲ US Army cipher cylinder, similar to the one invented by Thomas Jefferson. The 25 narrow wheels, each containing a jumbled alphabet, give millions of possible cipher combinations.

▲ An electric cipher machine, operated by a typewriter keyboard, invented by Edward Hebern, whose machines were used by the US Navy in World War Two.

	A	B	C	D	E	F	G	H	I	J	K	L	M	N	O	P	Q	R	S	T	U	V	W	X	Y	Z
A	A	B	C	D	E	F	G	H	I	J	K	L	M	N	O	P	Q	R	S	T	U	V	W	X	Y	Z
B	B	C	D	E	F	G	H	I	J	K	L	M	N	O	P	Q	R	S	T	U	V	W	X	Y	Z	A
C	C	D	E	F	G	H	I	J	K	L	M	N	O	P	Q	R	S	T	U	V	W	X	Y	Z	A	B
D	D	E	F	G	H	I	J	K	L	M	N	O	P	Q	R	S	T	U	V	W	X	Y	Z	A	B	C
E	E	F	G	H	I	J	K	L	M	N	O	P	Q	R	S	T	U	V	W	X	Y	Z	A	B	C	D
F	F	G	H	I	J	K	L	M	N	O	P	Q	R	S	T	U	V	W	X	Y	Z	A	B	C	D	E
G	G	H	I	J	K	L	M	N	O	P	Q	R	S	T	U	V	W	X	Y	Z	A	B	C	D	E	F
H	H	I	J	K	L	M	N	O	P	Q	R	S	T	U	V	W	X	Y	Z	A	B	C	D	E	F	G
I	I	J	K	L	M	N	O	P	Q	R	S	T	U	V	W	X	Y	Z	A	B	C	D	E	F	G	H
J	J	K	L	M	N	O	P	Q	R	S	T	U	V	W	X	Y	Z	A	B	C	D	E	F	G	H	I
K	K	L	M	N	O	P	Q	R	S	T	U	V	W	X	Y	Z	A	B	C	D	E	F	G	H	I	J
L	L	M	N	O	P	Q	R	S	T	U	V	W	X	Y	Z	A	B	C	D	E	F	G	H	I	J	K
M	M	N	O	P	Q	R	S	T	U	V	W	X	Y	Z	A	B	C	D	E	F	G	H	I	J	K	L
N	N	O	P	Q	R	S	T	U	V	W	X	Y	Z	A	B	C	D	E	F	G	H	I	J	K	L	M
O	O	P	Q	R	S	T	U	V	W	X	Y	Z	A	B	C	D	E	F	G	H	I	J	K	L	M	N
P	P	Q	R	S	T	U	V	W	X	Y	Z	A	B	C	D	E	F	G	H	I	J	K	L	M	N	O
Q	Q	R	S	T	U	V	W	X	Y	Z	A	B	C	D	E	F	G	H	I	J	K	L	M	N	O	P
R	R	S	T	U	V	W	X	Y	Z	A	B	C	D	E	F	G	H	I	J	K	L	M	N	O	P	Q
S	S	T	U	V	W	X	Y	Z	A	B	C	D	E	F	G	H	I	J	K	L	M	N	O	P	Q	R
T	T	U	V	W	X	Y	Z	A	B	C	D	E	F	G	H	I	J	K	L	M	N	O	P	Q	R	S
U	U	V	W	X	Y	Z	A	B	C	D	E	F	G	H	I	J	K	L	M	N	O	P	Q	R	S	T
V	V	W	X	Y	Z	A	B	C	D	E	F	G	H	I	J	K	L	M	N	O	P	Q	R	S	T	U
W	W	X	Y	Z	A	B	C	D	E	F	G	H	I	J	K	L	M	N	O	P	Q	R	S	T	U	V
X	X	Y	Z	A	B	C	D	E	F	G	H	I	J	K	L	M	N	O	P	Q	R	S	T	U	V	W
Y	Y	Z	A	B	C	D	E	F	G	H	I	J	K	L	M	N	O	P	Q	R	S	T	U	V	W	X
Z	Z	A	B	C	D	E	F	G	H	I	J	K	L	M	N	O	P	Q	R	S	T	U	V	W	X	Y

The Vigenère Square

In simple Caesar ciphers, each letter has the same cipher equivalent each time it is used. A 16th century Frenchman called Blaise de Vigenère developed the use of alphabet tables which made ciphers much harder to crack. The Vigenère Square is used with a "keyword" known only to the sender of a message and the person who receives it. The cipher for each letter changes each time the letter is used.

Here is an example of how to use the Square with a keyword. The message we want to send is SEND HELP NOW. We will use the word BOXER as our keyword.

Write out the message. Below it, write out the keyword BOXER repeatedly until you come to the end of the message:

Message: SEND HELP NOW
Keyword: BOXE RBOX ERB

Now turn to the table. Find the first letter (S) of the message on the alphabet at the top of the square. Then find the first letter of the keyword (B) in the key alphabet running down the left hand side. Now find in the table, the point where the column of letters running *down* from S and *across* from B meet. You will find that the letter is T. This is the first letter of the cipher.

Use the same method to find the next letter. Run down from E in the top alphabet to the point where it meets the O of the key alphabet. You will find that the letter is S. Now put the rest of the message into cipher in the same way:

Message: SEND HELP NOW
Keyword: BOXE RBOX ERB
Cipher: TS KH YFZM RFX

Cipher experts normally group their messages in regular clusters of, say, three letters to disguise the shape of their sentences. Grouping in threes, the final message reads: TSK HYF ZMR FX.

Deciphering

To decipher the message, write the keyword above the cipher message:

Keyword: BOX ERB OXE RB
Cipher: TSK HYF ZMR FX

Find the first letter of the keyword (B) in the key alphabet. Run *along* until you meet the first letter of the cipher (T). Now run *up* from the T until you reach the top alphabet. This gives S.

Keyword: BOX ERB OXE RB
Cipher: TSK HYF ZMR FX
Message: SEN DHE LP N OW

Problem: Solve the cipher below, using the method described. The keyword is TIMESPAN:

UMI EJT SRV ZQX ETS FTO QSF
EAT XAU BCT YJH ZPH SCG RK

▲ Lord Baden Powell, who set up the Boy Scout movement in Britain, was a spy during the Boer War. He posed as a butterfly collector, and sketched enemy fortifications while pretending to draw rare butterflies.

▼ The marks on the wings *between* the lines mean nothing, but those *on* the lines show the nature and size of the guns.

The position of each gun is at the place inside the outline of the fort on the butterfly where the line marked with the spot ends. The head of the butterfly points north.

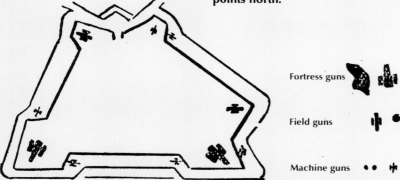

Fortress guns

Field guns

Machine guns

▶ An agent's miniature code-book (used by the Portland spy ring).

▼ "If necessary, eat your code-book!" Wise advice issued by the British in World War Two.

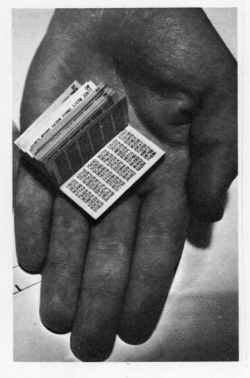

Cipher machines

Thomas Jefferson, the third President of the United States, invented a cylindrical cipher machine in the 18th century. But he filed away his notes on the subject and forgot about them. They were not found until 1922, the very year in which the US Army adopted a similar device, invented independently.

The invention of the telegraph and Morse Code boosted the study of ciphers, since enemy agents could easily tap telegraph wires and listen in on ordinary messages. Radio communication also encouraged developments. Machinery was used more and more to handle increasing volumes of secret correspondence.

In 1917, an American called Vernam invented a machine which could transmit telegraph messages and put them into cipher at the same time. The message was tapped out on a keyboard in the usual way while a random "key" was fed into the machine at the same time. At the other end, another machine stripped the message of the key, leaving the clear text. By World War Two, Allied cipher machines were handling some two million words a day, using models developed from Vernam's device.

"Scramblers" are telephone devices which work on similar principles. A device at one end of the line mixes the sound into garbled "grey noise", while the de-scrambler at the other end converts it back into ordinary speech.

"One-time pads"

Of course, spies operating undercover cannot carry bulky coding and decoding machines around with them. They still use simpler ciphers, or carry "one-time pads". These are tiny books consisting of sheets of cipher tables. The groups of figures are produced at random by a computer, and each cipher is used once only. Since the figures are arranged at random, it is almost impossible to crack the cipher. By the time such a cipher has been solved, the information may be worthless.

Newspaper codes

Spies sometimes put messages in the announcement columns of newspapers to convey a secret meaning according to some agreed plan. The simplest message, "Love and kisses—Peter," or "Welcome home—Paul" may hold a secret meaning. The advantage of this method is that the sender need have no contact with the receiver.

Wartime censors read all newspapers with care. In World War Two, British censors checked all cryptic crosswords and one censor took home a knitting pattern and made the garment to see if its design held a secret message.

Spies at Sea and in Space

Reference

ELINT

Exactly how useful are spies today? Many military leaders are suspicious of information which is obtained by human means. Even the most trusted agent may turn out to be working for the other side. The world of espionage is shadowy and uncertain. Leaders often prefer to rely on ELINT (Electronic Intelligence) reports brought in by spy planes, ships, satellites and submarines.

Aerial espionage

Planes were first used to fly over enemy lines and photograph their defences in World War One. During World War Two, RAF reconnaissance aircraft were used to find the exact location of German rocket sites (acting on information received from Resistance workers). By the end of the war, aerial espionage was well established.

But spy planes faced new problems. Radar detection was also developed in World War Two. In a way it provided a new and efficient counter-espionage service. Radar detection is based on the pulsation of radio waves which can be aimed up at the sky to rebound from any approaching aircraft.

The U-2 crisis

The first modern spy plane was the American U-2. It was designed to fly so high that it was beyond the range of enemy radar stations, and could pass unnoticed over its target area. It had special cameras with telephoto lenses, and operated at a height of over 20,000 metres. It was also equipped with a destruction mechanism which was activated if the pilot used his ejector seat.

On April 30, 1960, a U-2 plane was shot down while flying over Russian territory. The pilot, Gary Powers, had no time to operate his destructor. He himself escaped the crash and was arrested. His plane was recovered by the Russians.

The incident caused an international scandal. It was the first time that the Russians could prove that America was using "spies in the sky" over Russian territory.

Recent spy planes have become much more advanced than the U-2. They have also developed new ways of seeking out and avoiding enemy radar systems.

▲ The American SR-71 "Blackbird". The SR-71 is a high-speed spy plane which can fly at more than 3,000 kph.

It was originally brought in to replace the slower U2. Other modern spy planes include the Lockheed A-11 and EC-121.

THE U-2 CRISIS

"*The Colonel (Colonel Shelton) said that just in case anything should happen, he was giving me some packages with Soviet money and some gold coins, which I might use to bribe Soviet citizens to help me, if I needed help. They were put into my flying-suit pockets. He also had a silver dollar coin which he showed me which had a needle installed in it. He said that there was no danger because no USSR aircraft or rocket could get to my altitude, but in case something happened and I was captured, the needle contained poison and, if I was tortured and I could not stand it, I could use the needle to kill myself.*"
GARY POWERS (FROM THE TRANSCRIPT OF HIS TRIAL IN RUSSIA, AUGUST 1960)

▲ Gary Powers, pilot of the U-2 spy plane shot down over Russia. Powers was a US Airforce pilot who was also employed by the CIA. He escaped the crash and was put on trial. He was sentenced to 10 years imprisonment, but was exchanged for the Russian spy Colonel Rudolf Abel in 1962. He died in a helicopter crash in 1977.

The radar war

The American *Prowler* deliberately sets out to attract the attention of enemy radar stations, so that it can record where they are. It uses special equipment to "jam" the radar signal. Enemy missiles can, of course, home in on the jamming signal. But the *Prowler* then switches off its signal. It can project an image of itself which the missile will follow. Failing that, it can also drop "chaff" (metal shavings) which may confuse the missile even more.

Many planes carry complex radar equipment of their own to scan deep inside enemy territory. Unlike ground-based radar stations, they are not restricted by mountain ranges or the curvature of the earth. The British *Nimrod* can spot low-flying aircraft (another hazard for ground-based stations).

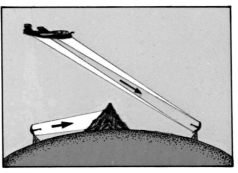

Spy satellites

The Americans sent up the first spy satellites in 1961. They were known as SAMOS (Satellite and Missile Observation System). They orbited the earth carrying powerful recording and photographic equipment. The film and recordings were dropped regularly by parachute and picked up in the Pacific Ocean by staff of NSA (National Security Agency).

The latest SAMOS satellite is called Big Bird. It is more than 16 metres long and three metres wide. Like earlier SAMOS models, it ejects film and recordings. But those of the Big Bird are caught in mid air by aircraft.

The Big Bird operates at a height of more than 160 kilometres. It is said that its cameras are so powerful that they can focus down on a man reading a newspaper in the street, and even give clear photographs of the text. Its listening equipment can pick up long distance telephone calls made on earth.

It might seem that with such equipment, spy satellites are invincible. But experiments are already being made with satellites capable of neutralizing the equipment aboard other satellites. Even in space, the perpetual duel between spy and counterspy continues.

◄ **Airborne radar can scan over mountain ranges. Some planes deliberately attract the attention of enemy radar so they can locate its position.**

Spies at sea

The fleets of the Eastern and Western worlds constantly patrol and manoeuvre in the oceans. While they perform their exercises, spy ships watch and listen.

Marine espionage first came to public attention in 1968. The North Koreans suddenly seized an American freighter called the *Pueblo* which was patrolling the waters near their coast. The *Pueblo* was a spy ship, known in espionage jargon as a "ferret ship".

It was an ordinary freighter, packed with sensitive listening devices. Its mission was to report on North Korean radio and radar communications.

The *Pueblo* carried antennae to find the direction from which radio signals were coming. It carried radar equipment to bounce messages off orbiting satellites. And it carried underwater hydrophones (listening devices).

After the *Pueblo* incident, the Americans stopped using ferret ships. But the Russians still employ them. Their spy ships are usually trawlers.

Today, spy submarines ("spook subs") patrol the underwater world. The great game of espionage is now played at a depth of several thousand metres.

MAIAKOVSKII TRAWLER

▲ **A shabby Russian trawler. Only the distinctive radar antennae give it away as a spy ship, or "ferret ship". Beneath** the surface of the water, it trails hydrophones to pick up underwater communication.

Ready Reference

Security and Intelligence Services

Below is a list of the main national security and Intelligence services. Simply speaking, "security" means counter-espionage at home.

"Intelligence" means espionage directed against other countries.

Britain
MI 5 (its name has been changed to DI 5, but most people still refer to it by its old name): internal security and counter-espionage.
MI 6 (now DI 6, and sometimes referred to as SIS—Secret Intelligence Service): Intelligence espionage abroad.
Special Branch: internal security, a branch of the police force which often works closely with MI5.

China
Cheng Pao K'o: security service dealing with counter-espionage against foreign agents.
Chi Pao K'o: internal security service.
CELD (Central External Liaison Department): foreign Intelligence.

France
DST (Direction de la Surveillance Territoire): internal security.
SDECE (Service de Documentation Extérieure et de Contre-Espionage): Intelligence.

Israel
Sherutei Habitahon (Shin Beth): internal security.
Mossad: foreign Intelligence.

Soviet Union (Russia)
KGB (Komitet Gosudarstvennoy Bezopasnosti): security and Intelligence. Since the days of the Tsar's Ochrana, the name of the Russian Secret Service has changed several times. From the revolution to the present day the names have been CHEKA, GPU, OGPU, NKVD, NKGB, MVD, MGB and KGB.
GRU (Glavnoye Razvedyvatelnoye Upravleniye): military Intelligence.

United States
FBI (Federal Bureau of Investigation): internal security service.
NSA (National Security Agency): security service involved in code making and breaking.
CIA (Central Intelligence Agency): foreign Intelligence service.

West Germany
BfV (Bundesamt fur Verfassungsschutz): internal security service.
BND (Bundesnachrichtendienst): Intelligence. In Nazi Germany, there were three main Secret Service Organizations: the *Abwehr* (traditional military Intelligence organization), the Nazi Gestapo (internal political security) and the Nazi SD (security service of the SS).

Spytalk

Agent in place: an agent who occupies a useful position (in the opposition's Intelligence service, for example).
Agent provocateur: an agent employed to stir up trouble in order to compromise the opposition
Bag job: breaking and entering.
Black operations: illegal operations, such as blackmail, kidnapping and assassination.
Bleep button: a small electronic device which can be planted on a car, or (more rarely) on an agent. It gives off a signal which can be tracked on a radar screen. Also known as an ESD (Electronic Surveillance Device).
Blown: an agent exposed as a spy is said to be "blown".
Bug: any small surveillance device, but usually a listening device.
Centre: the KGB headquarters, now situated in a modern complex of buildings south of Moscow.
Cipher: systematic rearrangement of the alphabet for secret writing.
Cobbler: a forger of passports. The passports are known as "shoes".
Code: words or symbols that have an agreed double meaning.
Company: CIA agents refer to the organization as the Company.
Cover: a false identity or false story used by a spy in his work. The word is also used for the day-to-day job of an agent whose main work is espionage.
Cut-out: a go-between, used to protect the identity of a spymaster from his agents. Cut-outs are often used to recruit new agents.
Dead letter box: a secret hiding place for messages which are to be picked up later. Also known as "dead drops", and, by the Russians, as "duboks".
Defect: to leave one's homeland and go secretly to a foreign country to betray secrets in return for safety.
Disinformation: the spreading of false information or propaganda in order to confuse or discredit the opposition.
Double agent: this term is generally used to mean an agent pretending to work for one side while really working for the other. It may also mean a freelance agent who sells information to both sides.
E and E: escape and evasion. An E and E specialist is an expert whose job is to rescue threatened or captured agents. (MI 9 was a British wartime agency specializing in E and E).
Embassy: most governments keep permanent representatives in other countries, to negotiate trade agreements and pacts, for example. These representatives live and work in an embassy inside the foreign country. Some of the embassy staff may be Intelligence officers.
Farm: the CIA training school at Langley, Virginia.
Field: a spy "in the field" is an agent on a mission in opposition territory.
Firm: British agents sometimes refer to their Secret Service as the "Firm".
Fumigating: checking premises for bugs.
Funkspiele: (German for "radio game") radio deception operations.
Illegals: trained agents working under false names and without diplomatic cover.
Lion tamer: a strong-arm man.
Measles: a murder victim whose death is made to appear accidental is said to have had "measles".
Opposition: modern Intelligence officers rarely speak of the "enemy". They refer to the "opposition".
Resident Director: the agent in charge of a whole country or group of countries.
Safe House: a hideaway for agents or defectors.
Soap: sodium pentathol, a truth drug.
Sleeper: an agent who does not operate until he can be of real use.
Spook: anyone professionally involved in espionage.
Y service: wireless deception

Further reading

Book of Secret Codes: F. Travis, Knight Books, 1977
Tales of Spies (Men): Jerrome, True Adventure Series, Blackie, 1970
Tales of Spies (Women): Jerrome, Blackie, 1970
The Masterbook of Spies: D. Mac-Cormack, Hodder, 1973
Neil Grant's Book of Spies and Spying: N. Grant, Kestrel, 1975
The Real Book of Spies: Epstein and Williams, Dobson, 1959
Real Life Spies: B. Newman, White Lion Publishers, 1974
Spies and Secret Agents: Winifred and Gillian, Kaye and Ward, 1977

For older readers
Secret Service: 33 Centuries of Espionage: Rowan and Deindorfer, Hawthorn, 1967
Encyclopaedia of Espionage: Ronald Seth, New English Library, 1972
Espionage: Michael Tregenza, Hamlyn, 1974
The Man From Moscow: Greville Wynne, Hutchinson, 1967
The Man Who Never Was: E. Montagu, Evans, 1953
Gehlen, Spy of the Century: E. H. Cookridge, Hodder, 1971

Spy Fiction

Legends about spies go back for centuries, but the first published story was *The Spy* by James Fenimore Cooper (1821), a story set in the American War of Independence.

The Secret Agent (1907) and *Under Western Eyes* (1911) by Joseph Conrad conjure up the seedy world of *agents provocateurs* of Azeff's time.

Espionage appears in *The Purloined Letter* (1845) and *The Gold Bug* (1843), short stories by Edgar Allan Poe, and in *The Naval Treaty*, a Sherlock Holmes adventure by Arthur Conan Doyle.

The tales of Sapper and William Le Queux are still popular, as well as the thrilling exploits of Richard Hannay, told in *The Thirty-nine Steps* (1915) and *Greenmantle* (1916), by John Buchan.

Many writers have been involved in spying, and draw on their real life experiences in their books. In *Ashenden*, Somerset Maugham used the cover name he actually had in the Boer War: "Somerville" is his hero's code-name.

Graham Greene worked under Kim Philby, as an intelligence officer in Section V of the SIS, and he features spying in several of his novels—*The Third Man, Our Man in Havana*, and *The Confidential Agent*, for example.

James Bond, agent 007, Ian Flem-

▲ A Russian agent picking up material left for him in a "dead letter box" (from a film provided by British Intelligence and shown on British TV).

ing's dashing but fictional hero, is based on a mixture of three real spies: Fleming himself, Sidney Reilly and Dusko Popov, a British agent of World War Two. Fleming worked in Naval Intelligence during the war.

In contrast to the glamour of Bond's world, the heroes of John Le Carré's novels live their lives in an atmosphere of fear, loneliness and danger much closer to reality. Plots of spy stories are often complicated, but Eric Ambler's *Epitaph for a Spy* is a good introduction to spy thrillers.

Writers of junior fiction are also attracted to espionage. Here are some titles:

The Stronghold: Mollie Hunter, Hamish Hamilton, 1974. A Stone Age spy story, set in the Orkney Isles.

The Marked Man: Aylmer Hall, 1967, a story set in Ireland in 1796.

Operation Skydrop: M. Brogan, Aidan Ellis, 1977.

Fly For Three Lives: A. Barry, Muller, 1975.

Index

The numbers in **bold** refer to illustrations.